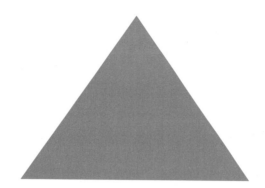

Your
Best Body Ever

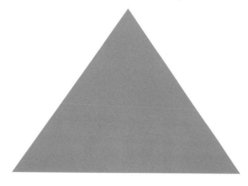

Anita Goa

McGraw-Hill

New York   Chicago   San Francisco   Lisbon
London   Madrid   Mexico City   Milan   New Delhi
San Juan   Seoul   Singapore   Sydney   Toronto

1 2 3 4 5 6 7 8 9 0 DOC/DOC 0 9 8 7 6 5 4

ISBN 0-07-142362-1

Printed and bound by RR Donnelley.

McGraw-Hill books are available at special quantity discounts to use as premiums and sales promotions, or for use in corporate training programs. For more information, please write to the Director of Special Sales, Professional Publishing, McGraw-Hill, Two Penn Plaza, New York, NY 10121-2298. Or contact your local bookstore.

This book is for educational purposes. It is not intended as a substitute for individual fitness, health, and medical advice. Please consult a qualified health care professional for individual health and medical advice. Neither McGraw-Hill nor the author shall have any responsibility for any adverse effects that arise directly or indirectly as a result of the information provided in this book.

 This book is printed on recycled, acid-free paper containing a minimum of 50% recycled de-inked paper.

I dedicate this book to my dad,
Rasmus Goa,
for trusting me enough to always say:
"Just figure it out. You can do it!"

Contents

Foreword

When Anita Goa first emailed me to ask if I would write the foreword for a book she was just finishing on a method of yoga and fitness called the "Goa system," I was intrigued. I know she's a good yoga teacher because not only did she work for me as a teacher for several years, where I had the opportunity to observe her teach, but I also was her teacher! Plus, she frequently sent her students to me for additional training and I'd hear wonderful reports from them about what a great teacher and person Anita was. Her students were well trained and well behaved, which also told me a lot about her as their teacher. However, while I knew that she was an outstanding yoga teacher, I didn't know anything about the "Goa system." When Anita sent the initial chapters, any reservations I had disappeared. I was completely captivated. This is great stuff, I thought to myself. The Goa system—a program combining yoga, aerobic training, and weight work—makes perfect sense and, further, is the ideal fitness balance we have all been striving and looking for.

For years, I've trained as a recreational athlete, at yoga and aerobics. I ran, biked, hiked, swam, and still do all that, only a little less frequently and vigorously now that I'm over 60! But I still enjoy aerobic training. Yoga, well, I've been doing that since 1971. I started practicing the astanga yoga program in 1980, named my contribution to the method "Power Yoga," and have been teaching it internationally since my first book, *Power Yoga*, was published in 1995. I never did weights, because I always figured that a strong yoga practice, like astanga, was enough.

I started teaching Power Yoga in New York City in 1980 through the New York Road Runners, and as the Wellness Director of the Club over the years have taught yoga to literally tens of thousands of runners and athletes of all types–cyclists, climbers, weight lifters, ball players, golfers, swimmers, skiers, boarders, etc. I have seen bodies of all types, sizes, and styles. I have seen what intense aerobic training can do to a body if that body isn't balanced with training in yoga. It gets tight! Very tight. And that usually leads to injury. I have also seen what lifting weights and only lifting weights does to a body if it isn't balanced with yoga—it gets tight, too. And injured. Over the years, we have had hundreds of endurance athletes and weight lifters in our yoga classes who came to do yoga because they were so "shut down" by their tightness that they could no longer access the strength that they worked so hard to build up. I know weight lifters and aerobic athletes need yoga!

Yoga, on its own, when practiced properly, can build strength *and* flexibility, as well as endurance, agility, and focus. It is also, in many cases, a form of physical therapy, and can heal and balance bodies that are sick, injured, or misaligned. So, theoretically, yoga should be enough. But ironically, almost all the yogis I know also run, walk, hike, swim, lift weights, bike, throw Frisbees, play rugby, climb mountains, or race sled dogs, among lots of other activities. They don't just sit in full lotus posture meditating on Divine Consciousness. Yogis, like everyone else, lift weights to build additional strength and run or bike or swim to develop additional endurance. Not to mention the fact that sometimes we do these things just because we like them! I walk and bike and swim not for any reason other than that I love to walk, bike, and swim.

The point is that, ultimately, many of us already try to cross train in some way and do all three—and if not three at least two—of these essential components of fitness and wellness. And if we aren't doing some aerobic training, some weight lifting, and some yoga, we should be. Your *best body ever* comes from a combination of endurance training, weight work, and yoga. The trick is finding the balance in an organized manner. Following the Goa system is surely one way to get it right.

Anita has spent years studying, training, and teaching aerobics, weight training, and yoga through the New York Sports Club, Road runners Club, Reebok Sports Club/NY, and Sports Club/LA in New York City, and through private one-on-one training and group classes. Her experience, enthusiasm, and guidance make her the ideal person to develop this program.

Oh, and one more thing. I like the way she writes. Anita grew up in Norway, and English is her second language. She has a unique and imaginative way of describing things. It's fun to read her stories and descriptions. The book is down-to-earth and refreshing.

And now, if you will excuse me, I've got to go. I'm starting my weight-lifting program, as incorporated with yoga and swimming, for my best body ever!

Beryl Bender Birch
East Hampton, New York
May 2004

An Attitude of Gratitude

I would like to thank:

My mom (Anne) and my dad (Rasmus) for never telling me what to do with my life, but trusting that I would make something of it.

Inger Juvastol, my teacher in 7th grade who put me in front of gym class and said, "Lead." I've been leading ever since.

Joan Levine, a wonderful client who guided me to her husband, Jim, my literary agent.

Jim Levine, who goes above and beyond literary agency. He never promises anything, but he delivers everything (and more). Levine Greenberg Literary Agency is an amazing office. Everybody has been so supportive of this book and my teachings. Thank you!

The team at McGraw-Hill: Phil Ruppel (Publisher), Lynda Luppino (VP of Marketing and Communications), Eileen Lamadore (Assistant Director, Marketing), Ann Pryor (Publicist), Arlene Lee (book design), Peter McCurdy (Production Manager), Nancy Hancock (Executive Editor) for believing in the idea and helping to shape the project, and Meg Leder (Associate Editor) for helping to complete it.

Beryl Bender Birch for showing me the power of yoga and for writing the foreword.

Elisa Cohen for the illustrations. Thanks for your patience in making sense of my stick figures!

Photographer Malachi Weir and assistant Pawel Litwinski for taking great photos. It was fun!

Jay Hachadoorian, my friend and a private trainer at the Sports Club/LA/NY for contributing his talent and amazing body for the photos.

Brian Cameron at Sports Club/LA/NY at Rockefeller Center for allowing us to use the club to take the photos of the machine weight exercises.

My sisters, Vivien and Jennifer, and all of my friends, students, and clients who have encouraged me a long the way.

Sanjay for loving me for the person I am and who inspires me every day to be the best I can be.

Having people around me who enhance my magnificence and support me when the going gets tough is priceless! Thank you all.

Love, Light and Eternal Happiness,

Anita Goa
New York City, July 2004

CHAPTER 1

Your Best Body Ever

Did you pick up this book because of the title? I'm glad you did. To me it's a sign that you're looking to improve your body, maybe lose some pounds, or reshape certain body parts. Perhaps you want to enrich your existing exercise program with yoga, get started with a balanced program of exercise, or feel better about yourself.

The Goa System is the first program for balancing the three elements of physical fitness—flexibility, strength, and endurance—using yoga as the foundation for a physical training regimen. It combines a series of yoga postures (asanas), weight training and aerobic exercise, and builds both your competency and your intensity levels as you progress through the program. Each level and every step is customized to meet your needs and lifestyle.

The Goa System will help you to become the best version of yourself that you can possibly be, whether you're a seasoned athlete or a fitness novice. This book presents alternate versions of every exercise so that wherever you start, you can feel successful as you work toward your goals.

Before I introduce you to the exercise routines of the Goa System, let me first tell you how I came to "discover" my own system and explain how it can help you get *your* best body ever!

My Journey to Fitness

I used to hate exercise. I don't mean dislike; I mean hate, as in never ever want to do it. When I was in elementary school in Norway, I forced my mom to write notes that would excuse me from gym class.

In return, I promised to do the dishes, laundry, or whatever she needed in the house, just so I did not have to sweat.

In a country where sports are a year-round way of life, I was a couch potato. You'd never catch me participating in any of the popular after-school activities such as cross-country skiing, soccer, or handball.

When I was 12 years old, my father sent me to spend the summer with friends outside of New York City. Every morning they tried to get me out of bed to join them in their Jane Fonda aerobics workout. But aside from hating to exercise, I loved to sleep. So I turned them down until I got so tired of being hounded that I gave in and tried it.

The moment I started doing aerobics, something clicked in my brain. This was great! I always loved music and dancing; in aerobics I could combine them both and it didn't feel like competition. I was immediately hooked.

My friends were stunned and delighted that they needn't beg to get me out of bed any more. But they were not nearly as stunned as my mother was when I returned to Norway: "No more excuses from gym class? Who is going to do all the housework?"

Not me! I was so hooked on aerobics that I began leading classes after school in my hometown. I was only 12 years old, but I was already beginning my career as a health and fitness instructor.

After college I moved to New York City and taught aerobics full-time. After five years of teaching twenty aerobics classes a week (plus extra running on the side) I was very skinny—and very exhausted. I was addicted to cardio! My male coworkers literally pulled me off the treadmill and urged me to start weight training and cut back on my aerobic exercise. They told me that adding weight training would help me build muscle mass, gain some pounds, and become better balanced. I figured it couldn't hurt, so I tried it—and it worked.

But something was missing. The whole idea of physical fitness, in my opinion, is to constantly challenge us to get better. I started to feel exactly the opposite. Instead of feeling replenished after my workouts I felt drained and burned out. I knew my body would be destroyed by the age of thirty if I kept teaching aerobics. I was praying for something else to come along. And as they say, when the student is ready, the teacher will appear: Beryl Bender Birch and Ashtanga Vinyasa

Yoga came my way. I said good-bye to aerobics and hello to practicing only yoga.

When I started yoga practice it challenged my strength, flexibility, and endurance in a way I had never before experienced. After yoga practice I was exhausted, but at the same time I felt grounded, centered, lengthened, expanded, rejuvenated, and relaxed. This amazed me; even though I always stretched and considered myself to be quite flexible, the yoga postures elongated me in different ways and helped my flexibility enormously (my muscles were very tight after all those years of teaching aerobics and step classes.) I had never felt refreshed in this way after a run or a weight-training session.

I started to play with an idea: What if I could feel the same way after a run or a weight-training workout, and how could I connect them while drawing the benefits from yoga into my aerobic workouts?

It didn't take long to notice that yoga went way beyond flexibility. Learning yoga breathing helped me sleep better. The concentration yoga requires helped me become more focused in those aspects of my life that lacked clarity. I not only had more physical energy, I had more mental energy and sharpness.

As I progressed to the advanced postures in ashtanga yoga, I realized I needed more strength in my arms. First I tried to increase my yoga practice and hold the positions longer, but that didn't work for me, so I started to incorporate weight training back into my routine. For variation, I added some aerobic workouts, though nothing like the level I had done before.

Soon I realized I was creating the ideal balanced fitness program—one that optimized strength, flexibility, and endurance.

My journey had brought me to use yoga as the foundation for an exercise program that incorporates other types of exercise, and it had taught me that yoga is a way of life.

Effects of the Goa System

I decided to try my integrated approach—what I had come to call the Goa System—with some of the clients I was coaching as a personal fitness trainer. If my client wanted to lose weight, but was only doing aerobics, I had her add yoga along with weight training, which is a more efficient way to convert fat to muscle. If he wanted to gain strength but was only doing weight lifting, I would have him incorporate aerobic exercise and yoga, to improve the client's balance.

I customized every client's exercise program because I understood through training different people that we all have different needs. It's important to be free to add the element you're missing and adapt the program to your own needs, goals, lifestyle, preferences, and body type.

When Frank came to me he was 40 pounds overweight and out of shape. He said if he could lose 10 pounds and keep it off, he would be the happiest man in the world. But with the Goa System, I knew he could do better than that. With a program adapted to his mental strengths—he was very goal oriented— he could lose all the weight he had gained, get fit, keep the weight off, and stay healthy.

When we started, Frank had very limited cardiovascular capacity and couldn't even do 10 push-ups. I taught him to do basic strengthening exercises so he could get a better feel for his own body, put him on a limited treadmill walking program, and to start him stretching I taught him the Sun Salutations ("These are actually fun," he said). Frank performed different elements of the Goa System on different days: some days he did free weight and machine weight exercises, some days he did run-walks, on some he just did yoga. However, he included yoga poses whenever he did weight training or aerobics. In the first six months, Frank lost 15 pounds. More important, because he found a balanced program that worked and that he enjoyed, he was able to stay with it.

Stacie was a voluptuous woman who had come to terms with her own weight but wanted to increase her overall fitness. She was very weak in strength and cardiovascular capacity, and had minimal flexibility. With Stacie, I created a program that included all three elements of the Goa System in every workout. Sometimes we would do 20 minutes of aerobic exercise, then 20 or 30 minutes of weight training, and finish up with 20 minutes of yoga. We'd vary the yoga poses depending on which muscle groups we'd worked in that session. The variation in the program kept it fun for Stacie so she kept at it.

Sarah was petite but disproportionate, with a top too small for her bottom. While she already did a lot of aerobic activity, she wanted to gain strength and get into better proportion. I had Sarah keep up her aerobic exercise but added the other two elements of the Goa System, weight training and yoga. After four months, her body was better balanced: she had gained strength and muscle in her upper body, downsized her hips, increased her flexibility, and made amazing increases in her aerobic capacity.

Yoga: The Foundation of the Goa System

One reason I felt so disconnected and got burned out in my early fitness routine was its purely physical approach. Creating the Goa System helped me find a foundation in yoga that provides far more than flexibility. Yoga provides an approach to life that opens the gateway to the full potential of our energy.

Yoga is often called a catalyst because it brings out the best in us; it doesn't bring out anything that's not already there. The word *yoga* means union, to join or yoke. It uses our attention to yoke the mind and body.

"Just working out" can be very draining. Other approaches to physical fitness work from the outside in, while in yoga we work from the inside out. I never realized this connection until I started practicing yoga.

When you make yoga the foundation of your exercise routine you work out with a purpose. The study of yoga builds a desire to integrate it as part of your life style. We practice yoga because it's a process. Each individual progressively builds strength, flexibility, and endurance according to his or her own ability and level.

Yoga was especially important as the foundation of Frank's program, because Frank tends to overdo things. So if he got into weight training or aerobic exercise, he might easily overdo, burn out, and quit. But incorporating yoga kept him balanced. In addition, Frank is a very busy executive and easily distracted. Yoga helped him to become more patient and to keep his priorities straight. The Goa System has become a natural part of his daily routine and it has changed his life. He lost more than 40 pounds, lowered his blood pressure, decreased his body fat, and got into better shape than when he played varsity sports in college.

Stacie, aside from losing weight, gained muscle and tone in her body, and her shape changed. She worked in the beauty industry and felt pressured to have plastic surgery, because she never felt pretty enough. Although she doesn't regret having her plastic surgery, she gained more confidence from working out than she ever could from going "under the knife." Yoga helped her from the inside out to deal with the fact that she was, as she put it, "always going to be a big girl" but to realize that she could still be in good shape and create her best body. Stacie changed so much that she switched careers and became a plus-size model! Isn't that beautiful?

Sarah is really disciplined, but thinks she never does enough. She loves hard physical work and enjoyed yoga because it challenged her but at the same time gave her balance and grounded her. The practice of yoga helped her get in touch with her body, and she started to become more aware of how she was punishing rather than nourishing herself through hard physical work. She realized she'd get better results by being kind to herself, while still getting the work done! This knowledge came in handy during menopause; she was more in tune with herself and could adjust better to the changes in her body and mind. Sarah also began to pay better attention to her eating habits, which happens naturally with this program. And because these changes come subtly, they don't feel restricting. She ate healthier and never felt better about herself or her body.

How to Use This Book

You don't need me as your personal trainer to use the Goa System. No matter what type of exercise you now do—or don't do—this book will show you how to incorporate the three elements of strength, flexibility, and endurance, while using yoga as the foundation for your physical fitness program.

Chapter 2 explains the design and benefits of the Goa System in more detail. It will help you understand why I use yoga as the foundation, and how all elements of the program work together to produce your best body ever. Even if you're tempted to jump to Chapter 3, where my actual program of exercises begins, I urge you to take the time to read Chapter 2.

The Goa System is divided into three levels, presented in Chapters 3, 4, and 5. You'll start at the one that matches your current level of activity or fitness and progress from there. In Chapter 6, I'll show you how to keep using the Goa System for the rest of your life, and how to customize it to your particular needs and lifestyle, but first I'll explain the three levels.

Level 1: This is where you should start if you haven't worked out in a long time or are not exercising regularly (at least two times each week). It's also where you should start if you are currently exercising but missing one or two of the elements of physical fitness: yoga flexibility, strength training, or aerobic exercise. Level 1 will help you integrate the three elements into a balanced program for optimal fitness.

Level 1 lays down a solid foundation. It will make you aware of all your body parts—what's strong and what's weak. It will teach you to connect your body into a whole unit, how to balance, how to breathe, and how to isolate and strengthen the major muscle groups.

Level 1 consists of three workouts per week, each lasting around 60 minutes. If you follow the program exactly, by the end of the month you will be ready to progress to Level 2. You should not progress to Level 2 unless you have done all of the exercises and yoga postures in Level 1 and feel comfortable with them.

Level 2: Start here if you have successfully completed Level 1 or if Level 1 doesn't feel challenging enough. This might be because you are already working out regularly at least twice a week, but make sure you are familiar with the yoga postures and strength training exercises from Level 1.

Level 2 builds on the foundation you established in Level 1 and is more challenging. You will become more comfortable with the yoga postures, breathing, and focus. You'll start using the stability ball for increased balance and core strength. And you'll increase the length and intensity of your aerobic activities.

Level 2 consists of four workouts a week, each lasting around 75 minutes. If you follow the program exactly, by the end of the month you will be ready to progress to Level 3. But don't rush to get to the next level; if you need more time, take it.

Level 3: Start here once you've successfully completed Level 2. By this time you should be comfortable with all the yoga postures and strength-training exercises.

Level 3 emphasizes strengthening each side of your body and getting your entire body into better balance. You'll perform more challenging exercises with the stability ball. And once again you'll increase the length and intensity of your aerobic activities.

Level 3 consists of five workouts a week, each lasting 60 to 75 minutes. If you follow the program exactly, by the end of the month you will be well on the way to having your best body ever.

Your Journey

As I discovered in my personal and professional journey, it's important to have the freedom to tailor all three elements of the Goa System to your individual goals and needs. By the time you have completed all three levels, you will have a good sense of whether you need more or less of one activity—yoga, strength training, or aerobics. You'll be able to customize your program to sustain your best body ever, according to needs and lifestyle, which I'll describe in Chapter 6.

Once you understand how to combine all of the elements of the Goa System, you won't have to do your program in a rigidly structured way. You'll be able to do a 30-minute workout if you don't have 60 minutes available, or three workouts a week if you don't have time for five. If you don't have a big block of time, you can do some exercises in the morning and some at night—whatever works for you!

Before getting to the actual program, let me explain in more detail what the Goa System is and how it can help you get *your* best body ever!

The Goa System

The Goa System is not "just" a yoga program or "just" a fitness program. It is a system that connects the three elements of physical fitness—weight (resistance) training for strength, aerobic exercise for endurance, and yoga for flexibility. Not only does the system connect the elements, but it shows how the elements complement each other. Both "yoga people" and "fitness people" will benefit from my program.

Think of the Goa System as a triangle. Yoga is the base (the foundation), and weight training and aerobic exercise are the sides.

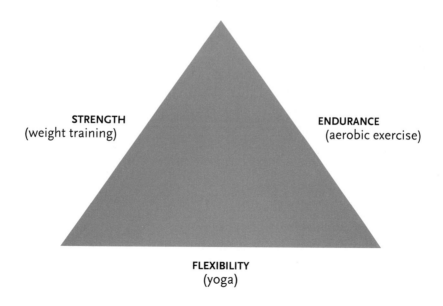

STRENGTH
(weight training)

ENDURANCE
(aerobic exercise)

FLEXIBILITY
(yoga)

Yoga is the base of the triangle because flexibility is the most neg-lected—and most vital—element of fitness. But each element is important for your body and your life.

Yoga Flexibility

Yoga is the most effective way to increase flexibility. By repeating the yoga postures over time, you will increase flexibility in every part of the body.

With age your body becomes tighter and the chances of injury increase. Moisture content in your muscle tissue decreases by about 15 percent as you grow older, and because of this, muscle fibers start sticking together and the elastic fibers get bound up with collagenous connective tissue, creating that "stiff" feeling. Stretching slows the process of dehydration by stimulating the production of tissue lubri-cants. Basically, stretching "creates" the water your muscle tissue needs to stay moist. In a sense, if you don't stretch you will "dry up," no matter how much water you drink. Incorporating yoga into your fit-ness routine helps slow down the process of dehydration by lubricat-ing your tissues.

Yoga postures were not invented to develop muscles or as a body-shaping system. But there is no doubt that yoga creates beautiful bod-ies. No matter what your build, yoga will elongate your muscles, making them longer and leaner.

Yoga affects weight loss because it is a mindful activity—you slow down and start to pay more attention to your actions by questioning: Do I really need that extra piece of cake? Am I really hungry now? Because the flexibility from yoga creates balance you let go of what you don't need. You eat from the inside, not from the outside.

The wonderful thing about yoga is that you begin to feel benefits immediately. You don't have to wait until your hamstrings are long or your body is "a certain way." You will quickly notice increased appre-ciation for and acceptance of your body.

Yoga is great for slowing down the aging process. Of course yogis age, but they don't grow old because there is constant re-newal. The practice is about connecting with yourself and finding (and trusting) your own path. If you pay attention, yoga will "create openings" and encourage you to become an optimal version of your self.

Here are the flexibility benefits yoga will give you at each level of the Goa System:

▲ Level 1: after four weeks you will start to stand taller and become increasingly aware of your breathing and body posture

▲ Level 2: after eight weeks your balance and energy levels will increase

▲ Level 3: after twelve weeks your body will be more flexible and balanced in a way it's never been before

Strength Training

Often people tell me, "Wow, you're strong, but you don't look it because you don't have big muscles." Most people associate strength with big bulky muscles and assume that the result of strength training is a body like Arnold Schwarzenegger's. Strength training doesn't necessarily give you bulk, but it will give you muscle—and you want muscle. The reason you want muscle is because, as you age, your:

▲ Metabolism slows down

▲ Lean muscle declines

▲ Body stores fat more easily

Having lean muscle mass keeps your metabolism active and steady, which in turn keeps your body from storing fat. Think of your body as a car where muscle is the engine, and fat is the fuel.

If you don't challenge your muscles, you could lose 5 pounds of muscle every decade after the age of 30 (during the menopausal years, it doubles!) The muscle you lose gets exchanged for fat. The key is to use the fat tissue as fuel by allowing the muscle tissue to expend it—both during activity and rest. This way, your body doesn't use the muscle and store the fat.

The good news is that you can reverse this process. By engaging in weight training your fat mass will decrease and your lean mass will increase. Muscles are toned, and your muscle "tone" refers to the muscles' firmness when you are at rest. The more muscle you have on your body, the more toned your body will look. Some people have more definition and/or more bulk, but that depends on how you work and how your body responds to the weight training. The Goa System will not bulk you up. Your body composition will change and you will become a lean-muscle fat-burning machine. As you begin to lose pounds, you will look like you've lost even more weight (and several dress sizes or belt notches) because muscle is more compact than fat, which is mushy, lumpy, and loose.

Research has shown that your metabolism stays active several hours after a strength-training workout and will burn about 25 percent of the total calories burned during the workout. Just 1 pound of added muscle from strength training can increase your resting metabolism and burn 30 to 40 more calories per day.

In the first three months of the Goa System you can add 3 pounds of muscle and start burning an extra 100 calories per day. You'll also be speeding up weight loss in the "problem areas" where fat seems to accumulate. For women, that's the upper arms (triceps), the hips, thighs, and buttocks; for men, that's the abdomen.

By doing some weight training you will reduce the damaging effects of gravity and aging. The resistance from weight training will push you into a different zone and allow you to keep moving forward, not relaxing into a decline. Here's what you can expect at each level of the Goa System:

▲ Level 1: after four weeks you will feel a change in your tone and strength

▲ Level 2: after eight weeks others will notice your "new body" emerging

▲ Level 3: after twelve weeks your body will be stronger in a more balanced way than it's ever been

Strength training together with yoga will give your body the proportion and balance it might lack. You're on your way to *your* best body ever!

Aerobic Exercise (Cardio)

Aerobic exercise such as running, step aerobics, cycling, or power walking is the best way to increase your endurance by making your heart pump more efficiently. Although aerobic exercise will contribute to weight loss, it's not the most effective way to maintain it. Yes, it burns calories efficiently, but it does not exchange the fat we burn with increased muscle like strength training does. You can easily burn five hundred calories in one session, but that's pretty much it. Endurance training does not increase your metabolism with a steady burn 24/7, as strength training does. Neither will it change your body composition profoundly. Endurance training is designed to keep your heart healthy, rather than rid your body of cellulite. Strength-training will "downsize" your thighs and keep them toned and relatively cellulite free.

If you don't overdo it, consistent aerobic exercise will give you stamina, vitality, and a great energy reserve. It contributes to a lower resting heart rate and will help decrease the risk of cancer and cardiovascular disease, the number-one killer in America.

As you progress through each level of the Goa System, you will experience increased benefits from your aerobic activity:

▲ Level 1: after four weeks you will feel your energy increasing

▲ Level 2: after eight weeks you will notice your stamina increasing

▲ Level 3: after twelve weeks, your energy and endurance will be better than ever before, and you'll be much less injury prone because of your strength and flexibility training

Each Element Enhances the Others

Obviously, any of the elements of the Goa System will give you benefits. But the effectiveness of the Goa System comes from the way each of the elements combines with the others to give you benefits way beyond performing each of them separately. Here's how:

▲ *Yoga flexibility enhances your strength training:* When your muscles lengthen they are better able to relax. You can't strengthen a tight or tense muscle. Whereas resistance exercises tend to isolate particular muscle groups, yoga stretching requires all muscle groups to work together as a whole—which is what you are ultimately trying to achieve in weight training.

▲ *Yoga flexibility enhances aerobic endurance:* Yoga postures stretch the overemphasized muscles you use in running, biking, or doing step aerobics. Improved flexibility helps you move more freely and prevent injuries. Moreover, the yoga practice teaches you to connect breath with movement, which helps you move more efficiently.

▲ *Strength training enhances yoga flexibility:* The benefit of getting physically stronger is stability—a combination of power, control, and improved muscular coordination. Strength training enables you to stretch further because the muscles are stronger. And strength training will give you the added muscle support you need to relax into each yoga posture.

▲ *Strength training enhances endurance:* The stronger and more flexible your muscles are, the more you're able to tolerate the "pounding" that comes with many aerobic activities. Resistance training will strengthen the underemphasized muscles you don't use as much. Strength training also works the anaerobic system. Working the anaerobic system with strength training helps your muscles to postpone lactic acid buildup.

▲ *Aerobic exercise enhances yoga flexibility:* Increased aerobic capacity together with deeper breathing helps you relax more, oxygenate the blood, and push the blood through the body more efficiently. The yoga flexibility practice in the Goa System is quite vigorous. This supplies enough oxygen to your muscles as they're being worked.

▲ *Aerobic exercise enhances strength training:* Increased aerobic capacity helps you breathe better and therefore delay lactic acid buildup in your muscles.

Why Yoga Is the Foundation

The Goa System is *inspired* by the practice of ashtanga vinyasa yoga. The underlying principles of ashtanga vinyasa yoga are to create dynamic movement according to your individual capacity and need while progressing toward a specific goal, in this case *your* best body ever!

The Goa System does not use the traditional sequencing of ashtanga vinyasa yoga since that is highly structured. But it does use the basic techniques: connecting breath with movement, working with proper alignment, and adapting to what you are able to do at any particular moment. This develops flow and creates integrated strength, flexibility, and endurance.

Below I explain the underlying principles of the Goa System—yoga flexibility, strength training, and aerobic activity—which you will find applied in each element of the program no matter what level you are working at (Level 1, 2, or 3):

- ▲ Optimal posture

- ▲ Breath-driven movement

- ▲ Focused awareness

- ▲ Flow

Let me explain each of them in more detail.

Optimal Posture

It's not easy learning alignment through a book, but as you practice and pay attention, you will learn what feels right. The Goa System's four alignment principles (ground, center, expand, and lengthen) will help you become more aware of the way you hold your body.

With each yoga posture, you'll find a photo of the "ultimate posture" to give you an idea of where you are heading. The stick figures show you the progression with modifications and breathing cues. (A modification is a version of the ultimate position that may be simpler for you to ease into as you work your way to the ultimate position. The breathing cues will help you determine how to best regulate your breathing. With some exercises, you may need to sustain an inhale or exhale through two positions. With others, you may need to inhale and then exhale, while still maintaining one pose.)

For the strength training exercises, you'll also find an ultimate position, as well as stick figures that show you the progressions and breathing cues. For the cardio, you'll find instructions for endurance activities and references to corresponding yoga postures.

Breath-Driven Movement

To breathe is to live and the better you breathe the more you expand life. Breath is life force or life energy.

A breath cycle consists of an inhalation (with a slight retention at the end) and an exhalation (with a slight retention at the end). The way you breathe has an enormous effect on your whole being. Shallow breathing is very taxing to the heart because it never gets a break.

When you breathe in full breath cycles and breathe with awareness (mindfully) you connect mind, body, and spirit into one unit, which makes it yoga. Mindful breathing calms your nervous system, slows your heart rate (giving the heart a rest), relaxes your body, releases mental congestion. By inhaling fully, you exchange carbon dioxide for new oxygen, and by exhaling, you let go of the carbon dioxide from your lungs. By breathing fully, you constantly supply your brain with oxygen to prevent fatigue and lethargy.

In all three elements of the Goa System, you connect your breath with the movement you are making; in this way, the breath becomes your guide. You don't breathe faster than you move, because you'll fatigue faster, and the same happens if you move faster than you breathe. Your goal is to make your breath deep and steady. Eventually the aim is to lengthen the inhalation and the exhalation as much as possible to expand your breathing and lung capacity.

In this calmer, more mindful state, you are better able to engage yourself and pay attention to how your work is affecting your body. In each level of the Goa System we cover several breathing techniques, such as free (belly) breathing, and ribcage (diaphragmatic) breathing.

T Y P E S   O F   B R E A T H I N G

Free Breathing

Lie on the floor on your back with both legs bent. Place the palms of your hands (lightly) on your belly. Keep your mouth closed, and breathe in and out through your nose. Take a couple of moments to observe what happens when you do this. Three things could happen:

1. Reverse breathing—when you inhale your belly goes in, and when you exhale your belly moves out (expands).
2. Chest breathing—your breath doesn't go to your belly, and it seems to stop at your chest.

   It is not beneficial to breathe either in reverse or do chest breathing, as they're very straining and extra work for the body.

   If you are breathing in either one of these ways, you want to make sure you reverse it to belly breathing:
3. Free (belly) breathing—when you inhale your belly should expand and when you inhale should return to normal.

   For Level 1, you're going to use this type of breathing.

Ribcage Breathing

For Levels 2 and 3, you'll move to a different stage of breathing: ribcage breathing.

Lie on the floor on your back with both legs bent. Place your palms lightly on your ribcage. Keep your mouth closed, and breathe in and out through your nose. Instead of letting the breath travel into your belly to inflate as you did in belly breathing, your belly will now be still and as you inhale your ribcage should expand, as if the ribs are moving sideways. You will notice your fingers moving away from each other. When you exhale they will return back to normal.

The diaphragm, the primary muscle of respiration, is designed to move up and down, and to billow sideways. When you inhale, the diaphragm moves down (to fill the lungs up with air), and when you exhale, the diaphragm moves up (to push the air out of the lungs). If you exhale fully, the inhale takes care of itself, because the exhale creates a vacuum that sucks the air naturally back into the lungs. So avoid forceful inhalations.

The benefit: In ribcage breathing the diaphragm gets strengthened and you're able to fully take advantage of your lung capacity by breathing deeper. Ribcage breathing activates the deep abdominal muscles and help give support to the lower back.

Focused Awareness

The practice of yoga teaches you to heighten your awareness of everything around you. In order to increase that awareness, you must learn to focus your eyes on a specific focus point (also called a *drishti*). A focus point is on or just beyond your body.

Because yoga is the practice of being mindful, it gives us plenty of things to pay attention to, such as where we place the feet, arms, pelvis, shoulders, neck, and head. By becoming more aware of how you move your physical body, you increase your level of focus.

The intention of a focus point is to draw the outward-looking eye inward. Using this discipline focuses the mind and takes you "inside"—it's a tool to help you be less distracted by external interruptions.

Flow

When ancient yogis looked at the animal world, they noticed how each part of animals' bodies moved in relation to another, each with a separate function but connected to an overall purpose. That is how they designed the yoga postures. Brilliant! The yoga postures help you connect disparate parts of your body into a functional and energetic unit. Learning to move as a unit allows you to work with good form (alignment) and will make your workouts more effective and efficient. When you do endurance and strength training, you want to make sure the body is working as an integrated unit and supporting your work.

Flow (vinyasa) is about creating movement according to your individual capacity and need. For example, if you can't do a full forward bend, you do a modified forward bend. The goal is to dynamically link postures with movement, while breathing and being aware of alignment as you improve your flexibility, strength, and endurance.

Flow has to do with the intensity and the progression of your workouts. It's important your body is able to support the intensity of the workout as you become stronger and more flexible. Making sure your body can support your intensity will help you progress in each element of physical fitness. Properly warming up and warming down (and stretching) your body after the workout are also key to progression.

Now you know in greater detail the underlying principles of the Goa System. Let me explain to you how breath-driven movement, focused awareness, and flow are incorporated into the three elements of physical fitness.

Building a Strong Tower from a Solid Foundation

YOGA FLEXIBILITY

1. BREATH-DRIVEN MOVEMENT

As mentioned above, your goal is to connect your breath with the movement you're making. There are basically three steps to yoga postures—moving into the posture, staying in the posture, and moving out of the posture.

You move into a yoga posture on a $^1/_2$ breath cycle, meaning you *either* inhale or exhale depending on what yoga posture category it is. Staying in the posture, you breathe full breath cycles, meaning you inhale and exhale, doing between five to ten breath cycles in each posture. You move out of the posture on $^1/_2$ breath cycle, meaning you *either* inhale or exhale depending on what yoga posture category it is.

When to inhale or when to exhale is always explained in the descriptions as well as how many breath cycles you should take in each posture.

Frequency

Flexibility is the most neglected element of physical fitness and the reason yoga is the foundation for the Goa System. By engaging in this program, you are making flexibility an integral part of your workout program. If you have a lot of stress in your life, it's necessary to release that tension on a daily basis, and yoga is one of the best ways to do this.

Duration

How long you should stretch depends on how much time you have. At minimum, you can do what is prescribed in the program and do the yoga postures that complement your strength training and aerobic exercise. Fifteen minutes can be enough if you are consistent, specific, and know what you want to accomplish.

~~~~~~

BE MINDFUL

▲ Equipment you need for yoga : Yoga block, yoga mat, strap (a towel works too).

▲ Get the fundamentals of each yoga posture first. Look at the pictures, read the general description, and try doing the posture. Use any modification so you adapt the yoga posture to your own body. Read the "focus on form" descriptions to take your practice further.

▲ Yoga is about balance and preventing injury. Injuries are often the result of forcing oneself into yoga positions without adapting, moving too quickly, progressing too quickly, doing too much too fast. Remember, there is no competition in yoga.

▲ Yoga is a process. If you have never stretched in your life, how can you expect it to happen right away? You have to earn it. Enjoy the moment, and practice patience.

▲ Yoga is done barefoot, so there is no need for shoes.

▲ Drink water pre-practice and post-practice. Try not to drink water during your yoga unless you are thirsty, a sign of dehydration. In yoga practice, you're working on an energetic level and constantly drinking water can affect that. If you notice you are frequently thirsty during your yoga practice, take note, maybe you're not drinking enough water pre-workout.

~~~~~~

3. Flow

Intensity

Intensity is different in yoga practice than in strength or aerobic exercise. You don't do sets or reps, or work within your Target Heart Rate Zone. Instead, you do each yoga posture one time on each side of your body. You hold each posture for five to ten breath cycles.

When you create flow you move dynamically with the yoga posture. Increased intensity is generally about moving deeper into the posture, not about moving faster in yoga practice. The goal is to "stretch your edge," which means that every time you practice you try to stretch yourself as far as you can in that particular moment without forcing or pushing yourself into it. Instead, you should use your breath to "get there." Movements should never be forced, but should flow smoothly.

You can determine your intensity by how you move out of a yoga posture. If you are straining, it's a sign you are working too hard. If you can move out of it with little energy, it's a good match. Remember, so you can reproduce it next time.

Ways to intensify your practice:

▲ Flowing from posture to posture

▲ Hold the yoga postures longer while breathing deeper

▲ Standing postures are more intense than seated postures

YOGA FLEXIBILITY FLOW

Just as there is a structure to follow in strength training, there is a structure in developing a yoga flexibility program. Here are some rules that are important to follow:

▲ The Sun Salutations are used as warm-ups and warm-downs.

▲ The standing postures are used as warm-ups and warm-downs.

▲ Pose and counter pose: After a back bending posture, counter pose with a forward bending posture. After a shoulder stand, counter pose with the Fish pose. After inversions like a hand stand, rest in the Child's pose for at least five breath cycles.

▲ Twists are encouraged before backward bends.

▲ Seated postures are used for flexibility at the end of the workout.

▲ Inversions like the shoulder stand are done after the seated postures (at the end of the workout).

▲ Final relaxation (Savasana) is done last for at least three to five minutes.

PROGRESS

You might feel you're not progressing as quickly in your flexibility as you are in your strength and aerobic endurance training. This is a natural feeling. One day you might be able to stretch further than another day. Think of it this way: You are "practicing yoga" and "it's just practice." This means we are serious about taking it lightly. The practice is a process and about *becoming* flexible.

You will notice progress in different ways: flowing more easily with the Sun Salutations, becoming more patient and tolerant of being uncomfortable while stretching, relaxing yourself into the process, letting go of the resistance you are feeling in your muscles by breathing, and becoming more aware of how your body is responding to being stretched in these various directions.

In the Goa System you will be shown the "ultimate" posture with modifications for each yoga posture for each level. You progress by being consistent and by adapting the yoga postures to what you are capable of doing at this moment. If you do that, then naturally, over time, you will progress from where you started to the "ultimate" posture.

The yoga postures become progressively more challenging as you move from level to level. You will find yourself progressing with the different levels of the Goa System. This doesn't mean that when you are done with a level you should be able to do the "ultimate" version.

STRENGTH TRAINING

1. BREATH-DRIVEN MOVEMENT

In strength training, a general rule is to exhale on the lifting movement (the contraction) and inhale on the lowering movement (the release). The breathing pattern is always emphasized in the exercise descriptions.

It's important not to do this in reverse or to work so hard that you don't breathe at all. Connect your breath with the movement you are making; don't hold your breath. Holding your breath while strength training causes tremendous internal pressure (because of the external resistance from the weights) and can limit blood flow to your brain and heart. Breathe continuously throughout every exercise set to avoid becoming lightheaded and increasing blood pressure.

You want to use Ribcage breathing when you strength train. It is OK to breathe out through your mouth, but make sure you breathe in through your nose.

2. FOCUSED AWARENESS

Frequency

The Goa System follows the American College of Sports Medicine's (ACSM) recommendation of targeting all major muscle groups at least two times a week.

You should not work the same muscle groups two days in a row, or do the same exercises for the same muscle groups two days in a row. When you strength train you should work your muscles to their max and then give them rest for at least forty-eight hours. You will work those muscles if you do your Sun Salutations the next day, but in a different way.

> *Warming-up for strength training:* Use the Sun Salutations and standing postures to warm up your muscles. The yoga postures in the warm-up phase prepare the muscles and skeleton for the work to come. The purpose of using the Sun Salutations as a warm-up is explained in the Level 1 yoga program.

> *Warm-down:* Use the seated yoga postures as part of the warm-down phase to elongate and counterbalance the impact the strength training (and aerobic exercise) has had on your muscles.

Duration

The duration of a strength training session depends on how many muscle groups you work, how many exercises you do for each muscle group, how many sets and reps you do, and how much time you rest in-between. In the three levels provided in this book you will be doing about thirty minutes of strength training. When you are ready to move beyond Level 3, or if you have more time on your hands, feel free to increase the duration of your strength training.

Be Mindful

▲ Equipment you need for strength training: body weight, tubing, dumb bells, bar bells, machine weights, and a stability ball.

▲ Execute all the strength training exercises with proper form (alignment).

▲ Execute all exercises with full range of motion. Full range of motion helps you improve your flexibility.

▲ Know what muscles each exercise is working. If you don't know what you are working and where the muscle is located, it's impossible to contract and isolate it.

▲ Give your body rest. It needs to get pushed, but at the same time it needs rest to get stronger.

▲ Drink water continuously during your strength training.

~~~~~~

3. FLOW

Intensity

In this program, as a beginner in Level 1, you will work up to twenty repetitions. (One rep means one repetition, which is a single contraction and release.) As you get used to that and gain a foundation, you'll work with twelve to fifteen in Levels 2 and 3.

In order to get stronger you have to constantly increase the load (also called overload). In weight training, we talk about "working to failure," which means you want to work the muscle within the set until you can't do a single repetition more. It stimulates your muscle to grow and get stronger. Overload has to do with the amount of weight you lift and how many times you lift it.

Research shows that moderate to slow exercise speeds are most effective for increasing muscular strength. This speed minimizes momentum, maximizes muscle tension, and decreases your risk of injury. Lifting movements of between two to four seconds are considered moderate. Lifting movements of five or more seconds are considered slow. I recommend you work with six-second repetitions, meaning you will use two seconds for the lifting movements and four seconds for the lowering movements.

One set is the number of reps you choose to do one after the other. We usually do between one to three sets for each exercise. In this program as a beginner in Level 1 you will work with one set, in Level 2 you will work with two sets, and in Level 3 up to three sets.

▲ Increase the weight, decrease the reps.

▲ Compound exercises like squat and lunges are more intense than isolation exercises like the leg extension and the leg curl.

▲ Rest less between sets.

▲ Perform two exercises back to back, usually chest/back, biceps/triceps.

▲ Perform one exercise after the other with little or no rest in-between each exercise.

―――――――――――――――――――――――――――――

PROGRESS

The whole point with growing and getting stronger is to progress. You can progress by adding more weight, more sets, more exercises, or more days (from two times a week to three).

Typically you want to increase the resistance by about five percent when you feel the load is getting easy. When you increase your load, decrease the repetitions and work yourself up to the reps again.

When you feel your muscles working better, you're able to isolate the targeted area better and your mental focus has increased. Knowing how hard to work yourself—what is enough (or not) is also progress.

AEROBIC ENDURANCE

1. BREATH-DRIVEN MOVEMENT

Remember that aerobic literally means *with oxygen*. It is important you breathe in and out smoothly during each aerobic exercise. Check that you are doing Ribcage (diaphragmatic) breathing. Work on keeping your mouth closed the whole time, but if you have to open your mouth, then inhale through your nose and exhale through your mouth. Slow down your intensity until you breathe properly.

Avoid rapid breathing. Start with a gentle pace where you can coordinate your breath to your activity. Work on coordinating your breath with your steps, exhaling and inhaling for an equal number of steps. Find a rhythm that works for you.

2. FOCUSED AWARENESS

Frequency

Perform at least two aerobic workouts a week to improve your cardiovascular fitness. Three sessions a week produces almost the same results as five. More is not necessarily better, unless you're a professional athlete.

Duration

Stay within a range of twenty to sixty minutes. Less than twenty minutes might decrease the benefit of your training. More than sixty minutes might increase your risk of overuse injury.

~~~~~~

BE MINDFUL

▲ Aerobic exercise is an activity that requires a combination of strength and flexibility. The impact affects your muscles and skeleton. It is very important to complement your aerobic exercise with strength training and yoga flexibility to enhance the efficiency of your aerobic workout and minimize musculoskeletal injuries.

▲ While performing your aerobic exercises, keep your focus in front of you. Try not to distract yourself by watching TV, or reading the newspaper or a magazine. Remember, your aerobic workouts should be just as mindful an activity as your yoga flexibility practice and your strength training.

▲ Pay attention to your form and to your intensity. Adjust yourself according to how you feel. Make sure you work within your Target Heart Rate Zone to get the most out of your workout.

~~~~~~

3. FLOW

Intensity

Exercise intensity is the level of effort at which you perform your aerobic activity. When you are starting out, and while building strength and increasing your flexibility, you should do activities that are low impact and high intensity so that your heart benefits, such as power walking and biking. When you've gained more strength and flexibility move into more high impact activities, like running.

A simple way to monitor your intensity is to use the "talk test." If you can talk normally the whole time you're exercising, your effort is probably too low. If you are able to speak in short sentences, your effort is probably moderate.

Another way to monitor your intensity is to find your Target Heart Rate Zone (THRZ). This is the zone where you will get the most out of your endurance workout. It should be an intensity you can keep for at least twenty minutes. If you work below your THRZ, you might not get full benefit of your workout. If you work beyond that level in every single workout, you might overwork yourself. The key is to stay within the zone.

General intensity rules:
For moderate exercise intensity: work at 50 to 70% of maximum heart rate
For vigorous exercise intensity: work at 70 to 80% of maximum heart rate

I suggest 50 to 60% for Level 1, 60 to 70% for Level 2, and 70 to 80% for Level 3.

For the most part we're going to work with a steady heart rate and on an aerobic level, with a little interval training on the anaerobic level.

Resting Heart Rate

Your Resting Heart Rate (RHR) and your Target Heart Rate Zone (THRZ) will help you monitor the intensity of your training and your aerobic fitness progress.

The purpose for taking your RHR is to determine how many times your heart beats per minute at rest. A normal pulse range for sedentary individuals is about 72 to 82 beats per minute (bpm). Your resting pulse lowers as your aerobic fitness increases. In fit individuals this pulse can be as low as 40 bpm. By knowing your resting pulse you can calculate your Target Heart Rate Zone.

All you need is a watch and your first two fingers (index and middle fingers). Do not use your thumb since it has its own little pulse which might distract you. You can either use the pulse on your wrist (the radial pulse) or the pulse on the side of your larynx (the carotid pulse).

Apply light pressure when you place your two first fingers on your pulse of choice. When you feel the pulse, start counting the pulse beats. The first beat is counted as zero, the second as one, and so on. Count for a full minute.

Do this for three consecutive days, and take note of the numbers by writing them down. For accuracy, take these measurements when you wake-up before you leave your bed, since your pulse can be affected by stress, coffee, exercise, and so on. Total the numbers for the three days and divide by three to get the average of your resting heart rate.

Target Heart Rate Zone

The purpose for knowing your THRZ is to find the pulse range (the intensity) you should be working at to increase your heart's fitness. The heart is a muscle, and like any other muscle, you have to put pressure on it for it to get stronger. However, you want to make sure you don't overstrain it; the THRZ ensures that you are working at a safe but effective intensity.

To determine your minimum and maximum zone, use the following equations:

220 – age = ( ) – RHR = ( ) x 50% = ( ) + RHR = Lower end of the THRZ

220 – age = ( ) – RHR = ( ) x 70% = ( ) + RHR = Higher end of the THRZ

Now you can find your training heart rate. Use the same procedure you did to find your RHR. This time, however, count for six seconds and add a zero to find your training heart rate for one minute. (You can also do it for ten seconds and multiply by six.)

Do this every ten minutes to ensure you are training in your zone. If it feels like this zone is too easy for you, adjust it until you find the intensity that's right for you.

Warming-Up

There are both physiological and psychological reasons you need to take time to warm up your body for the aerobic activity you're about to do. Warming up is about preventing injuries and giving your body the time it needs to get ready for the demands of the job that's ahead. The gradual progression toward your Target Heart Rate Zone will give you a safety measure, as well as gradually increasing your heart rate, metabolism, blood pressure, oxygen consumption, dilation of the blood vessels, elasticity of the active muscles, and the heat produced by the active muscle groups.

The length of the warm-up phase is up to you. Some people (myself included) take longer to warm-up, to adjust and kind of "get in the groove" than others. But you should definitely use at least three to five minutes to gradually warm-up.

Warming-Down

Most books call this phase a cool-down, but I like to think of it as a warm-down phase. Since you're still going to be doing the yoga flexibility work and strength work after the aerobics, it's important to not cool down completely so that you don't injure yourself.

The warm-down is the warm-up in reverse. A warm-down phase after aerobics will slowly decrease your heart rate and overall metabolism; prevent sudden pooling of blood in the veins; ensure adequate circulation to the skeletal muscles, heart, and brain; and prevent or delay muscle stiffness, muscle spasms, or cramping.

If you stop all of a sudden without warming down you might experience dizziness and/or post-exercise fainting (not a good experience!). If you are at high risk of cardiovascular disease it is absolutely crucial you gradually decrease the intensity. When you do aerobic exercise, the body releases exercise hormones like adrenaline to the blood stream. If you stop suddenly, the concentration of adrenaline in your blood can put too much pressure on your heart.

The length of your warm-down phase depends on the length of your work-out, but after a twenty to thirty minute workout, you should warm-down for at least three to five minutes. Adding the yoga stretching and weight training afterwards will help your body warm-down even more.

Pulling It All Together

By now I hope you understand all of the separate elements of the Goa System, how they work together, and the principles that will inform each element across every level. But if they still seem somewhat like bits and pieces, let me assure you that once you start following the program, you will begin to *feel* – in your body – how it all fits together.

Now you're ready to get started on the path to your best body ever, beginning either with Level 1 or Level 2, depending on your own level of fitness and activity.

Enjoy the journey!

CHAPTER 3

Welcome to Level 1

Level 1 is where you should start if:

▲ You haven't worked out in a long time but want to get back into the best shape of your life

▲ You are not currently exercising regularly—at least two times each week

▲ You are currently exercising but missing one or two of the elements of physical fitness: yoga flexibility, strength training, or aerobic exercise

▲ You want to learn how to integrate the three elements of physical fitness into a balanced program for optimal fitness

This first level of the Goa System will create your foundation for flexibility, strength, and endurance:

▲ The yoga flexibility postures in this level are basic and very easy to learn. However, they should not be underestimated since they will teach you to become aware of your breath and body posture. In this level you will practice free breathing (belly breathing). The yoga postures will also ease your body into stretching in different directions if you're not used to stretching, while making you more aware of your flexibility, balance, and strength.

▲ The strength training exercises will teach you proper technique and alignment while working with exercise tubing and your own body weight. They will also help you isolate and strengthen all of your major muscle groups. If you are having a challenging time with the yoga postures like Plank pose and Chaturanga—all of the strength training exercises in this level will help make your body more stable and stronger, so over time these postures become easier.

▲ The aerobic exercise program will set you off on the right path toward better aerobic endurance. You can choose between activities like power walking, biking, or doing group exercise classes like dance aerobics and step aerobics.

To do the Level 1 program, plan to do three one-hour workouts per week. The charts below give you guidelines for which exercises to do and for how long. Follow the 4-week program structure provided for this level. Within the general guidelines adjust to a Level 1 activity, intensity, and duration that works for you and your lifestyle.

Yoga Flexibility Program

YOGA POSTURE CATEGORY	YOGA POSTURE	REPS EACH SIDE/BREATH CYCLES/TOTAL APPROX. TIME
Warm-Up/Warm-Down	*Sun Salutation A*	2–4 reps/ $1/2$ breath cycle for each yoga posture, except 3–5 breath cycles in Downward-Facing Dog/ 5 minutes
Standing Balancing		
On both feet		
Side lateral bend	*Triangle pose*	1 rep/5 breath cycles/1 minute
Twist	*Rotated Triangle pose*	1 rep/5 breath cycles/1 minute
On one foot	*Tree pose*	1 rep/5 breath cycles/1 minute
Seated		

Yoga Flexibility Program (*Continued*)

YOGA POSTURE CATEGORY	YOGA POSTURE	REPS EACH SIDE/BREATH CYCLES/TOTAL APPROX. TIME
Forward bending	*Reclined Extended Hand to Big Toe pose*	1 rep/5 breath cycles/1 minute
	Child's pose	1 rep/5 breath cycles/30 seconds
Twist	*Reclined Spinal twist*	1 rep/5 breath cycles/2 minutes
Backward bending	*Half Frog pose*	1 rep/5 breath cycles/2 minutes
	Locust pose	1 rep/5 breath cycles/30 seconds
Relaxation	*Savasana*	3–5 minutes

Strength-Training Program

EQUIPMENT	BODY PART	EXERCISE	SETS/REPS/APPROX. TIME
Body weight	Legs	*Squat*	1 set/20 reps/1 minute
		Lunge	1 set/20 reps/2 minutes
		The bridge support	1 set/20 reps/2 minutes
Machine		*Leg press*	1 set/20 reps/2 minutes
Body weight	Core	*Basic Crunch*	2 sets/10 reps/2 minutes
		Oblique Rotation	2 sets/10 reps/2 minutes
Tubing	Chest	*Standing Chest press*	1 set/20 reps/2 minutes
	Back	*Standing Row*	1 set/20 reps/2 minutes
	Bicep	*Standing Biceps curl*	1 set/20 reps/2 minutes
	Triceps	*Standing Triceps kickback*	1 set/20 reps/2 minutes

Endurance program

EXERCISE	TIME
Power walk/run	20–30 minutes
Biking	20–30 minutes
Step aerobics, dance aerobics	Usually 45–60 minutes with warm-up and warm-down, plus core work

The 4-week program structure

Day	1	2	3
Structure	Cardio, Yoga, Legs, Chest, Biceps, Triceps, Core	Yoga, Core	Cardio, Yoga, Legs, Chest, Biceps, Triceps, Core
Yoga Flex			
	Sun Salutation A	Sun Salutation A	Sun Salutation A
	Tree pose	Tree pose	Tree pose
Cardio	Your choice		Your choice
Strength			
	Squat	Bridge support	Squat
	Lunge		Lunge
	Standing Chest press		Standing Chest press
	Standing Row		Standing Row
	Standing Biceps curl		Standing Biceps curl

(Continued)

The 4-week program structure (*Continued*)

Day	1	2	3
	Standing Triceps kickback		Standing Triceps kickback
Core	Basic Crunch	Basic Crunch	Basic Crunch
	Oblique Rotation	Oblique Rotation	Oblique Rotation
	Locust pose	Locust pose	Locust pose
Yoga Flex			
	Reclined Extended Hand to big toe pose	Reclined Extended Hand to big toe pose	Reclined Extended Hand to big toe pose
	Reclined Spinal Twist	Reclined Spinal Twist	Reclined Spinal Twist
	Half Frog pose	Half Frog pose	Half Frog pose
	Child's pose	Child's pose	Child's pose
	Savasana	Savasana	Savasana

Level 1 Yoga

THE SUN SALUTATIONS

The Sun Salutations are a dynamic group of yoga postures that form the foundation for the yoga program in the Goa System. You're going to learn two versions of the Sun Salutations. In Level 1 you'll practice Sun Salutation A, and in Level 2 you'll practice Sun Salutation B. In Level 3 you'll combine them and learn how to intensify them.

There are many dimensions to the Sun Salutations, so you'll learn something new in each level of the program. They might seem challenging at first, but take your time and practice them posture by posture, over and over again; soon they'll feel as natural as brushing your teeth.

The Sun Salutations are multifunctional. They will benefit you in many ways. They can be a workout by themselves, a great way to start the morning, or a help to wind down after a hectic day at work. They increase awareness of mind, body, and spirit; your sense of well-being; and good health.

You can use the Sun Salutations to warm up before your cardio and weight-training workouts. As you stretch, they increase the body's core temperature (they create heat); they oil the joints, draw the attention to the rhythm of the breath, reawaken the spine, and integrate the body as a whole. Use them to warm down after your cardio and weight-training workouts, since they stretch and strengthen muscles that are overused or underemphasized. The Sun Salutations help remove carbon dioxide from the lungs and replace it with fresh oxygen. They remove lactic acid buildup in your muscles so you'll feel less (or not at all) sore the next day. After a workout you'll be refreshed due to all the oxygenated blood in your brain, and you'll also feel mentally more clear.

Enjoy rising with the sun!

SUN SALUTATION A

You are now going to go through a sequence of 14 positions to learn Sun Salutation A. These positions involve different categories of yoga postures, such as standing postures, forward bending postures, and backward bending postures. I'll explain each one as I present it.

Each position and category will teach you something new about your body: where you are strong and where you are weak, where you are limber and where you are tight, and so on. I show the "ultimate" pose and always give modifications. It's important to experiment with the postures so you can customize them to your present level and ability. Remember, it's about what you can do now. Grow from where you are, not from where you think you should be. Just get an idea of where you are heading and work yourself in that direction.

First familiarize yourself with the individual postures, then "try them on" by breathing in them and feeling the position that is comfortable. When you feel at ease work on connecting the postures. Last, connect the breath with the movements.

Enjoy the moment; before you know it you will be flowing through the positions!

Attention Pose (also called Mountain Pose)

Benefits: I call the Attention pose the "perfect posture" pose because it integrates all the muscles in the body. This pose will increase your awareness of how to position your skeleton and improve your posture as well as your energy level. Try to stand in this position for about 3 minutes; you'll notice where your muscles are tight and weak.

Attention pose strengthens: Upper back (teres major, trapezius), belly (transverse abdominis), erector spinae, quadriceps, buttocks, ankles

Attention pose stretches: Hip flexors, front shoulders, chest, belly (transverse abdominis)

Complementary yoga postures: Upward-Facing dog, Cobra, Locust pose.

Complementary strength exercises: Leg press, basic crunch, standing row

Exhale

Stand with your feet together and parallel, hands together at your heart center. This prayerlike position is also called *Namaste* (I salute the Divinity within me from the Divinity within you). Keep toes spread and feet grounded onto the floor, and quadriceps contracted.

FOCUS ON FORM

Breath/Focus: When moving through the Sun Salutations you will exhale into the pose. When standing in the position breathe freely in and out. Gaze at a point in front of you.

Ground: You are grounding from your feet.

Center: Your pelvis is in a neutral position, where your tailbone "drops" down and your belly is engaged.

Expand: Be sure to lift your breast bone and to relax your shoulders away from your ears, rolling them back and engaging your upper back muscles. You will feel an openness in your heart and lungs.

Lengthen: You are lengthening through your spine from your tailbone to the crown of your head.

Arm Raise Pose

Benefits: Arm Raise pose is primarily a flexibility pose. This pose lifts us up, drawing the energy up. It also releases tension in the shoulders and chest and stimulates the abdominal organs, diaphragm, and heart.

Arm Raise pose strengthens: Core (transverse abdominis and erector spinae), quadriceps, buttocks, ankles

Arm Raise pose stretches: Chest, upper back (latissimus dorsi), shoulders, triceps

Complementary yoga postures: Downward-Facing Dog

Complementary strength exercises: Same as for Attention pose. Wide pull-ups incorporate the same movement and build both strength and flexibility. You don't need to be strong to be able to raise your arms above your head. It's more about flexibility.

From Attention pose inhale and raise your arms perpendicular to the floor with arms either shoulder-width apart or palms joining. Tilt your head back and gaze at your thumbs. You can adjust the arms according to how your shoulders feel. Make sure your body position is not affected by raising your arms. Exhale into Standing Forward Bend.

FOCUS ON FORM

Breath/Focus: Inhale into the pose, exhale out of it.

Ground: You are grounding from your feet. Keep toes spread and feet grounded onto the floor, and quads contracted.

Center: You are centering though your pelvis. Keep your pelvis in a neutral position the entire time. Make sure you don't arch your lower back when you raise your arms.

Expand: You are expanding through your rib cage, so make sure that as you raise your arms, you keep your breastbone lifted, with your shoulders away from your ears. This way you can fully inhale and feel openness in your heart and lungs.

Lengthen: You are still lengthening through your spine, from your tailbone to the crown of your head.

STANDING FORWARD BENDING POSTURES

Forward bending postures are in general considered passive; gravity is used to stretch the muscles of the back of the body—the spine, hamstrings, and calves. They help release mental and physical stiffness and tension from a stressful or inactive lifestyle, so forward bends can be both relaxing and energizing at the same time.

Modification

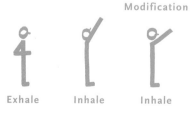

Exhale   Inhale   Inhale

On a different level an inability to bend forward might show a stubborn personality, and is also associated with fear. Forward bending can help release the fear of being "back-stabbed"; let go of the fear and release the necessity to control what we might need to leave behind.

Forward bends compress and massage the abdominal organs (liver, kidneys, pancreas, spleen, and intestines) and stretch the spine. They help maintain the natural curve and length of the spine by separating the vertebrae. This is important as we age, to avoid shrinking and bad posture. Forward bending also stimulates the nerves along the spinal column and improves circulation around the spine. They will prevent you from stagnating or growing old or narrow minded; think about letting go of what you don't need to carry, so you can travel lightly.

In the Goa System you will practice both standing and seated forward bending postures. We start with the Standing Forward Bend.

In the Standing Forward Bend you ground from the feet. It's important to:

▲ Bend (hinge) from the hips and lead with your belly and heart. This gives greater flexibility of movement and creates a stronger pressure against the abdomen.

▲ Never force the spine farther forward than your hamstring flexibility allows. If your hamstrings and lower back are tight, use the modifications. With time and the help of gravity your hamstrings will lengthen, but in the meantime make sure you keep yourself lifted to create space to fully exhale as you bend forward—it encourages the muscles you are stretching to lengthen.

▲ To create length in your spine you must expand through your rib cage. Engage your belly, lift your breastbone, relax your shoulders, draw your shoulder blades together, and keep your head lifted. If you constantly hunch that's how your spine will grow and it will counteract what you are trying to accomplish.

Standing Forward Bend

Benefit: Standing forward bend is mostly a flexibility asana. Bending forward releases tension from the muscles in the back of the body.

The blood flow to the head and brain both ener-
gizes and calms the mind.

Standing Forward Bend stretches: Hamstrings,
calves, spine (lower, middle, and upper back)

Standing Forward Bend strengthens: Quadriceps,
latissimus dorsi, trapezius, core (transverse
abdominis)

Complementary yoga postures: Downward-Facing
Dog, Reclined Hand to Big Toe Posture

Complementary strength exercises:
Leg press

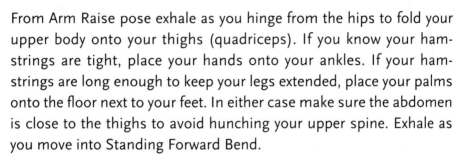

From Arm Raise pose exhale as you hinge from the hips to fold your
upper body onto your thighs (quadriceps). If you know your hamstrings are tight, place your hands onto your ankles. If your hamstrings are long enough to keep your legs extended, place your palms
onto the floor next to your feet. In either case make sure the abdomen
is close to the thighs to avoid hunching your upper spine. Exhale as
you move into Standing Forward Bend.

FOCUS ON FORM

Breath/Focus: Exhale into the pose. Gaze at the floor.

Ground: You are grounding from your feet. Keep toes spread and feet
parallel and grounded.

Center: The pelvis naturally rotates back to accommodate the forward
bending movement. Make sure your belly is engaged to protect the
lower back.

Expand: Even when folding over the thighs, make sure to keep the
breastbone lifted, enabling you to maintain extension through your

Modification

Exhale   Inhale   Exhale   Exhale

upper spine. This allows you to feel the openness in your heart and lungs and be able to fully exhale and empty the air out of the lungs.

Lengthen: You are still lengthening through your spine (even if you are lengthening your hamstrings) Keep the spine long whether your legs are straight or bent.

Halfway Pose

This pose is often cited as "look up and lengthen" or "prepare" before stepping back into Low Lunge and Plank pose.

Benefit: Halfway pose is mostly a flexibility pose. It's a great precursor for deeper backward bending postures such as Upward-Facing Dog and Locust pose. It helps improve your posture by keeping the spine supple and strong and improving circulation in the lower back region, and relieves fatigue by toning the spinal nerves. It will improve your inhalations by creating more space in your rib cage to open the lungs and heart. This helps to create renewed energy.

Halfway pose stretches: Chest, core (rectus abdominis), spine (lower, middle, and upper), front of the neck, hamstrings, calves, biceps, shoulders

Halfway Pose strengthens: Quadriceps, shins, toes, upper back (latissimus dorsi, trapezius), back of the neck, core (transverse abdominis, erector spinae).

Complementary yoga postures: Downward-Facing Dog, Upward-Facing Dog

Complementary strength exercises: Leg press, Standing Row

Modification

Exhale   Inhale   Exhale   Inhale   Inhale

From Standing Forward Bend, inhale as you lift your torso and head to extend your spine and look forward. Depending on where your hands are in the Standing Forward Bend, either place your hands on your shins or lift onto your fingertips (keeping the fingertips next to your toes). Exhale as you move into Low Lunge.

FOCUS ON FORM

Breath/Focus: Inhale into the pose and gaze at a point in front of you without straining your neck muscles.

Ground: You are grounding from your feet. Keep feet parallel and together with toes spread.

Center: You are centering through the pelvis, make sure to keep the belly engaged to give support to the lower back as the spine lifts and extends.

Expand: As the spine extends lift the breastbone, relax the shoulders, and roll the shoulders open to make room for a deep inhalation.

Lengthen: You are lengthening from your tailbone to the crown of your head.

Low Lunge

Benefit: This is both a strength and flexibility pose. Low Lunge is a good precursor to more challenging arm balances such as Plank pose. It teaches precision in placing the arms and legs in the right place and balancing the interaction between the front and back body muscles while practicing full body integration through the hands and feet.

Low Lunge stretches: Chest, shoulders (front), biceps, neck (front), core (rectus abdominis), and the extended leg: quadriceps, hip flexor, calf, ankle

Low Lunge strengthens: Upper back (trapezius, rhomboids, serratus anterior), core (transverse abdominis), triceps, wrists, hands/fingers, and the bent leg: quadriceps, buttocks, shin, ankle, foot

Complementary yoga postures: Plank pose

Complementary strength exercises: Leg press, lunge

From Halfway Pose keep looking forward and exhale as you step your right leg back into a lunge position. Place your palms shoulder-width apart on either side of your bent left leg. Your left knee is parallel with your ankle. Fully extend your right leg from your hip in order to get extension throughout your body. Inhale as you step your left leg back into Plank pose.

FOCUS ON FORM

Breath/Focus: Make sure you fully exhale into the pose. As you step the leg back into the lunge, keep your visual focus in front of you as you extend your mental focus to all parts of your body, making sure you are fully extending yourself.

Ground: You are grounding through your feet and hands. Your front foot is parallel to your back foot and all toes are spread. You're on the ball of your right foot. Keep your right leg extended and contract the right quad as you press back through your forefoot. Feel the full extension from hip joint to heel.

Center: Your pelvis should be moving into a neutral position; the belly is engaged and active to avoid sinking in your lower back.

Expand: Keep your breastbone lifted to expand your chest. To accomplish this, you might need support through your fingertips or to use yoga blocks rather than keeping your palms on the floor.

Modification

Exhale   Inhale   Exhale   Inhale   Exhale   Exhale

Lengthen: Don't drop your head; keep it lifted without straining the neck muscles. Feel the extension from your right heel through your body to the crown of your head.

ARM BALANCING POSTURES

Arm balancing postures are more fully addressed in Level 2. Plank pose and the yoga push-up Chaturanga are your first taste of what's to come in the arm balance category. Arm balancing postures are about developing both mental and muscular strength and full body integration. A very important ingredient is having fun with them. The more you practice, the better and stronger you'll get! If you find you are weak in Plank pose and Chaturanga use the complementary strength-training exercises to help you gain more strength and stability for the next level.

If you find your wrists are weak or in pain from practicing the arm balancing position, you might find relief in a foam-covered yoga prop called Gripitz. This prop was designed for this purpose. Check resource page for details.

Enjoy, have fun, and be serious about taking these poses lightly!

Plank Pose

Benefits: Plank pose is primarily a strength pose. It integrates the body into a whole and balances the interaction between the front and back body muscles. This helps to develop a sense of inner equilibrium and harmony.

Plank pose stretches: Front shoulders, chest, and hip flexors; it's primarily a strength pose and no real flexibility is needed.

Plank pose strengthens: Upper back (upper/middle/lower trapezius, rhomboids, latissimus dorsi), triceps, entire core, quadriceps, forearms, wrists, hands, fingers

Complementary yoga postures: Downward-Facing Dog, Chaturanga (yoga push-up)

Complementary strength exercises: Leg press, standing row, triceps kickback, biceps curl

From Low Lunge inhale as you step your left leg back into what feels like a push-up position. Keep your focus on the floor in front of you. If you find that you sink into your lower back, lift the hips up to maintain full extension. If your head drops, lift your head. Your arms may be too weak to support yourself in the Plank pose. If so, work with one leg at a time until you've developed enough strength. Exhale as you lower into the yoga push-up (Chaturanga).

FOCUS ON FORM

Breath/Focus: Fully inhale into this pose. If you can't, adjust your body until you can. Draw your awareness particularly to the lower back and neck. Think Attention pose on your hands and feet.

Ground: You are grounding through your hands and feet. Keep your fingers and toes spread. Press the palms of your hands into the floor.

Center: It is extremely important you engage your core muscles in this position to avoid sinking in your lower back.

Expand: Keep the breastbone lifted, relax the shoulders, and draw the shoulder blades together. Allow the back muscles to support you. Keep your heart and lungs open so that you can breathe fully.

Lengthen: Start by feeling the extension from your tailbone through your spine to the crown of your head. Then feel the length from your heels to the crown of your head.

Modification Modification

Exhale   Inhale   Exhale   Inhale   Exhale   Inhale   Inhale   Inhale

The Yoga Push-Up (Chaturanga)

Benefit: The yoga push-up is primarily a strength pose. Everyone loves to hate it, but think positively! It develops full body integration, a super strong upper body, a strong mind, and improved self-image. If you can do the yoga push-up, you can do practically anything.

Chaturanga strengthens: Upper back (upper/middle/lower trapezius, rhomboids, serratus anterior), biceps, core (transverse abdominis, erector spinae), quadriceps, forearms, wrists, hands, fingers

Chaturanga stretches: Chest, shoulders (front), ankles, feet, toes

Complementary yoga postures: Plank pose, Cobra pose

Complementary strength exercises: Standing row, biceps curl, leg press, basic crunch

From Plank pose exhale as you lower your chest toward the floor until your shoulders, elbows, and hips are in one line. Unless you're using a modification, the only body parts touching the floor are the palms of your hands and balls of your feet. Keep your gaze in front of you toward the floor. Inhale as you move into Upward-Facing Dog.

FOCUS ON FORM

Breath/Focus: Fully exhale as you lower yourself into the position. If you have trouble with this, you need to modify the position. Draw your mental focus away from the floor and pay attention to how your body is responding. Act accordingly!

Exhale   Inhale   Exhale   Inhale   Exhale   Inhale   Exhale   Exhale   Exhale

Ground: You are grounding through the palms of your hands and the balls of your feet.

Center: Your core is strongly involved in order to keep the pelvis in place, protecting your lower back.

Expand: Feel the integration and relax your shoulders by keeping the breastbone lifted and shoulder blades drawn toward each other.

Lengthen: You are still lengthening through your spine, from your tailbone to the crown of your head, but you will also feel extension from your heels to the crown of your head.

Upward-Facing Dog

Benefit: Upward-Facing Dog is both a strength and flexibility pose. It helps improve posture by keeping the spine supple and strong. This pose increases circulation in the lower back region and relieves fatigue by toning the spinal nerves. Upward-Facing Dog also stimulates digestion and relieves constipation.

Upward-Facing Dog strengthens: Upper back muscles (trapezius, rhomboids, serratus anterior, latissimus dorsi), triceps, shoulders (rear), core (transverse abdominis), forearms, wrists, hands, fingers, quadriceps, buttocks, calves.

Upward-Facing Dog stretches: Shoulders (anterior), chest, spine (lower, middle, upper), belly (rectus abdominis), shins, toes

Complementary yoga postures: Cobra pose, Locust pose

Complementary strength exercises: Standing row, Standing bicep curl, Standing triceps kickback, basic crunch

From Chaturanga there are two options to move into Upward-Facing Dog.

The first option is what I call "manual" moving. From Chaturanga position first point the right foot and then the left foot (you'll be on the tops of your feet). Press your palms against the floor and inhale as you push yourself forward and up into Upward-Facing Dog.

The second option is to roll over the toes—it doesn't hurt and will not break your toes!. From the Chaturanga position push away from the toes so you start moving forward, then press the palms against the floor as you inhale and lift into Upward-Facing Dog.

Keep your focus forward.

Whether you use the "manual" or rolling option, make sure your lower back is protected as you push yourself into the Upward-Facing Dog. If it's too much for your back to fully extend the arms, then practice Cobra pose. Exhale as you move into Downward-Facing Dog.

FOCUS ON FORM

Breath/Focus: As you move into the position it's important to maintain your ability to fully inhale. Adjust your range of motion according to the length of your inhalation; in other words, if you can't inhale all the way into the Upward-Facing Dog (the breath stops halfway there), you might be better off modifying to Cobra pose. As you become accustomed to practicing backward bending your inhalations will lengthen and you will naturally progress to the Upward-Facing Dog pose. Keep your focus forward, and do not throw your head back.

Ground: You are grounding through your arms and the tops of your feet. Keep the quadriceps active to avoid collapsing into your ankles or lower back.

Center: Keep your belly engaged to keep the pelvis in as neutral a position as possible to avoid "crunching" up the lower back.

Expand: It's important you push your hands against the floor so you get lift through your torso. This way you can keep your breastbone lift-

Modification

Exhale   Inhale   Exhale   Inhale   Exhale   Inhale   Exhale   Inhale   Inhale ed, relax the shoulders, and roll the shoulders back to draw your shoulder blades together.

Lengthen: You are lengthening from your feet (the tops of your feet) to the crown of your head Visualize yourself balanced like a suspension bridge.

Cobra Pose

Benefit: Cobra pose is both a strength and flexibility pose. It's a yoga pose by itself, but it can also be a modification of Upward-Facing Dog and offers the same benefits.

Cobra pose strengthens: Upper back muscles (trapezius, rhomboids, serratus anterior, latissimus dorsi), triceps, shoulders (rear), core (transverse abdominis, erector spinae), forearms, wrists, hands, fingers, quadriceps, buttocks, calves

Cobra pose stretches: Shoulders (anterior), chest, spine (lower, middle, upper), core (rectus abdominis), shins, toes

Complementary strength exercises: Triceps kickback, standing/seated row

Complementary yoga postures: Bow, Camel, Fish, Wheel variations

From (your version of) Chaturanga lie face down on your belly. Your hands are under your shoulders and your arms are bent. Lift your head and look forward as you lift your torso as far off the floor as you can, with arms slightly bent. Press your hands against the floor and lift your torso. Keep your legs hip-width apart and toes pointed.

Modification

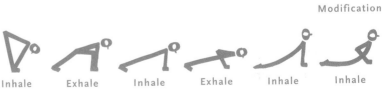

Exhale   Inhale   Exhale   Inhale   Exhale   Inhale   Exhale   Inhale   Inhale

What is inhibiting you from moving into Upward-Facing Dog pose? It can be weakness in your arms or tightness in the spine, neck, shoulders, and/or lower back. By practicing the Sun Salutations, you will increase your muscle strength and grow more limber in your spine. If you have experienced any disk problems, you should avoid Upward-Facing Dog and stay with Cobra pose.

FOCUS ON FORM

Breath/Focus: Inhale as you lift into the pose. Keep your gaze at a spot in front of you.

Ground: You are grounding through your pelvis and hands. Keep palms grounded and fingers spread.

Center: Keep your pelvis in a neutral position (by "tucking" your tailbone under) and your belly active.

Expand: Keep the breastbone lifted as you move into the pose to draw the shoulder blades together and keep your shoulders away from your ears.

Lengthen: You might feel resistance in your lower spine, but make sure you don't feel pain. Avoid throwing your head back. This allows you to feel the extension from your tailbone to the crown of your head.

Downward-Facing Dog

Benefit: Downward-Facing Dog is both a strength and a flexibility pose. In this position the circulation in the upper spine is stimulated and the nerves in the spine are toned, particularly in the upper spine. This pose helps calm the brain and relieve stress and, at the same time, energize the body.

Downward-Facing Dog Pose strengthens: Upper back (teres major, trapezius, serratus anterior, latissimus dorsi), triceps, forearms, wrists, hands, fingers

Downward-Facing Dog stretches: Spine, chest, shoulders, hamstrings, calves, achilles, feet, neck (rear).

Complementary Yoga postures: Arm Raise pose, Plank pose

Complementary strength exercises: Rotator cuff exercises, standing row, triceps kickback, biceps curl

To get into Downward-Facing Dog pose you follow the same movement that you did moving from Chaturanga to Upward-Facing Dog pose; either roll over the toes or go back "manually." From Upward-Facing Dog pose, exhale as you lift your hips to the sky into an inverted V position, your Downward-Facing Dog position. Your arms are shoulder-width apart and your legs are hip-width apart. You want length in your spine. Feel the weight moving toward your heels.

If you find your spine rounds when you extend your legs, modify your position by bending your legs to maintain the extension in your spine. You might be able to extend your legs more as you warm up—over time these muscles will lengthen. Hold Downward-Facing Dog for 3 to 5 breath cycles.

In the beginning, Downward-Facing Dog pose is quite challenging, but as you get used to it, it becomes a restorative posture—I promise.

FOCUS ON FORM

Breath/Focus: Exhale into Downward-Facing Dog and hold the position for 3 to 5 breath cycles. Draw your chin toward your chest and gaze toward your navel.

Exhale   Inhale   Exhale   Inhale   Exhale   Inhale   Exhale   Inhale   Inhale

Modification Modification

Exhale/Inhale   Exhale   Exhale
3–5 ×

Ground: You are grounding with both hands and feet. Keep your fingers spread and press your palms against the floor. It is not imperative that your heels touch the floor, but it is important to bring your weight back into your heels to avoid resting all of your weight on the upper body.

Center: In this position the pelvis is tilted forward; keep your belly engaged to support your lower spine.

Expand: As you press your palms against the floor, draw your shoulders away from your ears, keep your breastbone lifted, and draw the shoulder blades into your back to maintain extension in your upper spine.

Lengthen: It's important that you feel the length in your spine. If your legs are extended, you will feel the length in your hamstrings.

Completing Sun Salutation A

From Downward-Facing Dog pose, you'll rewind the postures back to Attention pose. Inhale step right leg forward to Low lunge, exhale step left leg forward, inhale to Halfway pose, exhale to Standing Forward Bend, inhale to Arm Raise pose, exhale to Attention pose.

| Exhale | Inhale/Exhale | Inhale | Exhale | Inhale | Exhale |

STANDING POSTURES

Balancing on Both Feet

The standing yoga postures are an extension of the Sun Salutations and are also great for warm-ups and warm-downs for your strength training and aerobic exercises.

The standing yoga postures represent a balance of muscular strength and endurance, flexibility, balance, full body integration and a sense of being, and becoming grounded. The standing postures are very moving and energetic, and they create a lot of heat. They will increase your awareness of how you carry yourself and improve your physical balance by developing the brain center that controls how the body works in motion.

The standing postures involve balancing on both feet in side lateral bends and twists, plus balancing on one foot.

Most people don't think of "balance" when both feet are grounded. The Triangle pose and Rotated Triangle pose might change that thought. Although these postures give you a wide base to work from they are still challenging because bending sideways or twisting gives you a different sense of balance. The aspects of centering, expanding, and lengthening while breathing and trying to stay relaxed add a different element than standing erect.

In standing postures you ground from the feet (or foot). It's important to:

▲ Be aware of how you position your feet and spread your toes to avoid gripping the floor (it doesn't help balance)

▲ Engage the front of your thighs (quadriceps)

▲ Keep your pelvis in a neutral position and engage your belly to give support to your lower spine and center the body

▲ Lift your rib cage and relax your shoulders so you can breathe fully

▲ Draw your shoulder blades together to give support to the upper spine and to create length in your whole spine

▲ Gaze on a spot in front of you

▲ Not be afraid to lose your balance. The more you fall over with awareness the more balance you will gain. Just fall gracefully.

If you find yourself very wobbly and weak use the complementary strength exercises. If you find yourself tight, use the complementary yoga postures to help you improve.

STANDING SIDE LATERAL BEND AND TWIST

So far you have become more aware of how your body has responded to standing erect (Attention pose), bending forward (Standing Forward Bend pose, Downward-Facing Dog pose) and bending backward (Halfway pose, Upward-Facing Dog pose).

Now you'll practice bending sideways and twisting. Bending your torso sideways stretches your hips, lower back, waist, and the muscles between your ribs (the intercostals). This will increase and sustain your energy level, relieve back pain, and improve your breathing.

The core is particularly involved in side bends and twists. The abdominal muscles are strengthened and stretched, so your abdominals become sleeker and stronger than ever. The added flexibility and strength of the deep abdominal muscles will enable you to breathe more fully and balance better. The bending and twisting will help create more space between the intercostal muscles for your lungs to expand and this will help increase your breathing capacity. Digestion and constipation are often improved as well. Twists enhance energy around the navel and will tone, detoxify and nourish the internal organs.

The side lateral bending and twisting postures usually work together as pose and counter pose. They lengthen, strengthen, and balance the muscles along your spine. The spinal nerves are both stimulated and calmed down. If you find you lack core strength use the complementary strength exercises mentioned under each posture.

Are there any knots in your life? When twisting, visualize wringing them out, so while ridding yourself of knots you are gaining energy. Who said you can't do two things at the same time? Welcome challenges as an opportunity to connect and grow.

Triangle Pose

Benefit: Triangle pose is both a strength and a flexibility pose. It improves your balance and stretches the intercostals (muscles between the ribs) which help deepen the breath.

Triangle pose strengthens: Front leg: Feet, ankles, quadriceps, inner thigh, buttocks; plus, obliques, quadratus lumborum, upper back (trapezius, rhomboids), core (transverse abdominis)

Triangle pose stretches: Back leg: Inner thighs, hips, core (obliques, quadratus lumborum, intercostals), latissimus dorsi, chest, front shoulders, hamstrings, ankle

Complementary yoga postures: Extended Side Angle pose, Side Plank pose

Complementary strength exercises: Oblique rotations, stability oblique bend

From Attention pose, step your left leg behind you (approximately $3^1/_2$ feet). Keep right heel inline with arch of left foot. Open your body sideways and face the side. Extend your arms to shoulder height. Exhale as you stretch over your right leg and lower your right hand to your right shin or ankle, while reaching your left hand to the sky. Inhale as you turn your head and gaze in the direction of your left fingertips. Hold for about 5 breath cycles. Inhale to a vertical spine and exhale to Attention pose. Repeat on your left side.

FOCUS ON FORM

Breath/Focus: Make sure to execute full breath cycles while in the pose. Keep your gaze focused upward on your fingertips while extending your awareness to all parts of your body.

Ground: You are grounding from the feet. Keep your toes spread and your quadriceps active.

Center: Your pelvis must be in line with the legs and torso. If the buttocks are then pushed back, pull them back in. Keep your belly active.

Expand: The breastbone is lifted, shoulders relaxed, and shoulder blades contracted. Feel an expansion through your heart center.

Modification

Exhale   Inhale   Exhale   Exhale   Inhale   Exhale

Lengthen: You are lengthening from your tailbone to the crown of your head, but also lengthening through the arms. Your arms should feel as if they are being pulled in opposite directions.

A COUNTER POSE

There is nothing haphazard about the structure of a yoga practice. A counter pose is used to balance the previous pose. After a side lateral bend we counter pose with a twist. After a backward bend we counter pose with a forward bend.

Rotated Triangle Pose

Benefit: Rotated Triangle pose improves your balance and stretches the muscles along the spine independently to improve balance. This pose significantly stimulates the nerves along the spine. Rotated Triangle pose gives you energy, tones the belly, and stimulates the internal organs. Opening the chest in this pose helps improve breathing.

Rotated Triangle pose strengthens: Quadriceps, inner thigh, outer thigh; plus core (obliques, transverse abdominis, internal organs, diaphragm), trapezius

Rotated Triangle pose stretches: Hamstring, hip, core (obliques, transverse abdominis), latissimus dorsi, chest, shoulders, biceps

Complementary Strength exercises: Oblique rotations, lunge twist

Modification Modification

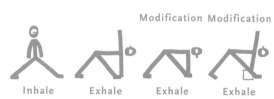

Exhale   Inhale   Exhale   Exhale   Exhale   Inhale   Exhale

Complementary yoga postures: Reclined Spinal Twist, Fierce Twist

From Triangle pose inhale as you square off your hips to the right without moving your feet. You can narrow your stance if you find it challenging to balance, but your feet must to be in the same 90- and 45-degree positions. Then exhale as you extend your left arm to the ceiling while keeping your right arm alongside of your body. Inhale as you reach forward to lower your left palm to a yoga block or to the floor on the small-toe side, and exhale as you extend your right arm toward the sky and look in the direction of your right fingertips. If you can't ground the palm to the small-toe side, try the large-toe side, or hold onto your ankle. Think Triangle pose in reverse.

Hold the pose for 5 breath cycles. Inhale as you rewind back to starting position. Exhale into Attention pose.

FOCUS ON FORM

Breath/Focus: It is more challenging to breathe when balancing and twisting at the same time, but make sure your breath is with you throughout and don't go further than what you feel your breath can support. Stretch your gaze beyond the fingertips and feel yourself becoming more and more stable as you are twisting and reaching at the same time.

Ground: You are grounding from your feet, making sure your feet don't move the entire time. Keep your toes spread and your quadriceps active.

Center: Keep your pelvis stable by engaging your belly to create support for your lower spine. It's important to rotate into the pose from your midback (the bottom of your ribs) and not from your hips.

Expand: The more grounded and engaged your legs and abdomen are, the more you can lift your breastbone, relax your shoulders, and draw your shoulder blades together to get extension in your upper spine. This will help with the twisting and with breathing.

Lengthen: You are lengthening from the tailbone to the crown of your head, evenly through both arms.

BALANCING ON ONE FOOT

Balancing on one leg adds another degree of balance. When we lack balance we must compensate to avoid falling over. This imbalance creates a lot of strain on the body, and can often lead to discomfort, pain, and injuries. By practicing all these postures you give your body a chance to regain its natural balance and you gain a sense of feeling more free, graceful, and fluid.

By improving your balance you are better able to conserve energy. This is an important aspect of yoga practice, and the essence of energy management. Why use more energy than you must? At the end of the day you'll still have energy left, so you can do the things you want to do feeling energetic and full of life.

Balancing on one foot might be challenging at first, but with practice you will progress quickly.

Tree Pose

Benefit: Tree pose is a little bit about strength and flexibility, but mostly about balance and full body integration. It will teach you that balance has nothing to do with being stiff and rigid, but is all about being rooted and finding your center. Within the stillness of the pose there is room for "movement." Literally visualize yourself as a tree, root yourself and branch out; come what may, you'll just sway with it in complete balance.

Tree pose strengthens: Standing leg: foot, ankle, shin, quadriceps, buttocks; plus core (transverse abdominis, erector spinae), upper back muscles (trapezius, rhomboids)

Tree pose stretches: Inner thigh, hip, and ankle. Chest, front shoulders

Modification

Exhale   Inhale   Inhale/Exhale   Exhale   Inhale/Exhale

Complementary strength exercises: Leg press, lunge

Complementary yoga postures: Attention pose

From Attention pose, draw your right knee to your chest, open the knee to the right, and place the sole of your right foot onto the inside of your left thigh. Press the foot against the thighbone to help establish your balance. Don't press the foot against the knee joint!

Place your hands in prayer position in front of your heart. Keep your focus on a spot in front of you. As you first try this pose, hold it for 5 breath cycles. As you improve and you can hold comfortably for 10 breaths, begin to extend your arms to be perpendicular to the floor. Tilt your head back and look toward the sky. Once you have mastered this move, try to balance with your eyes closed—it's possible! Open your eyes and exhale as you return to Attention pose.

FOCUS ON FORM

Breath/Focus: Breathe deep, full breath cycles in the pose. Focus in front of you, to the sky, and move your awareness throughout your body.

Ground: You are grounding from your left foot. Keep the left foot parallel (no turning out or in) and balance evenly on the foot. Contract the left quadriceps.

Center: Keep the pelvis in neutral so you feel length in your spine, and keep your belly active.

Expand: Lift your breastbone and draw your shoulder blades into your back. Relax the shoulders.

Lengthen: You are lengthening from your pelvis to the crown of your head.

SEATED POSTURES

Most of the seated postures in Level 1 are reclining postures, but I still consider them seated postures.

The seated/reclining postures are less physically demanding on your balance and strength than the standing postures. Reclined postures are really great because you don't have to use too much strength to sit upright; you can relax and pay attention to alignment, flexibility, and breathing.

Since they are more "relaxing" you can stay in these poses and gain more lasting flexibility. Even if you are already flexible, you can work on strength, alignment, and breathing. This will help you as you move into Level 2.

SEATED FORWARD BEND

The seated forward bending postures have the same benefits as the standing ones. The only difference is that less balance is required when seated and you are grounding from the pelvis instead of the legs. If your hamstrings, hips, and spine are stiff it can be challenging to create length in the spine while bending forward. Starting off with a reclined version of a seated forward bend gives you a chance to feel the length of your hamstrings while relaxing your spine and breathing fully. This will help you move into deeper and more challenging forward bending postures in Level 2.

Reclined Extended Hand to Big Toe Pose

Benefit: Reclined Extended Hand to Big Toe pose is similar to a pose that you will learn in Level 3—the Standing Extended Hand to Big Toe pose. This one requires less balance than the more advanced pose. The reclined version will provide an awareness of your hamstring flexibility and will keep your body balanced while in a reclined position, which can be a challenge.

Reclined Extended Hand to Big Toe pose strengthens: Quadriceps, shin, ankle; plus core (transverse abdominis), upper back (trapezius, rhomboids), biceps

Reclined Extended Hand to Big Toe pose stretches: Hamstring, inner thigh, buttocks, calf, ankle

Complementary strength exercises: Leg press

Complementary yoga postures: Standing Forward Bend pose, Standing Extended Hand to Big Toe Pose

Recline on the floor. Inhale as you wrap a yoga rope (a towel works, too) around your right flexed foot and exhale as you extend the leg as far as your hamstring will allow. Draw the extended leg toward your chest, keeping your right quadriceps contracted. Keep your left leg extended on the floor. Keep the quadriceps contracted and use it as an anchor. If you are flexible take hold of your right big toe with your two first fingers and thumb.

Hold the pose for 5 to 10 breath cycles. Inhale. Place your left hand on your left hip, and exhale as you open the right leg to the side while making sure the left hip stays down. Open the leg as far to the side as will allow your pelvis to stay grounded. Stay open to side for 5 to 10 breath cycles. Inhale, lift the right leg back up, and exhale as you lower the leg to the floor. Repeat using the left leg.

FOCUS ON FORM

Breath/Focus: Breathe deep and gaze toward the sky as you focus your awareness on how your body responds to the pose. Be mindful of your alignment.

Ground: Your foundation is your pelvis, spine, and leg. Feel the leg extended to the floor as if it is an anchor stretched from the hip to the heel.

Modification   Modification

Exhale/Inhale Exhale/Inhale Inhale/Exhale Inhale/Exhale

Center: Keep the pelvis in a neutral position, making sure you feel length through your lower spine. Keep your belly engaged to keep the body from moving back and forth.

Expand: As you extend each leg further or draw it closer to your body, keep your shoulders relaxed by lifting your breastbone and rolling your shoulders back.

Lengthen: You are lengthening from your tailbone to the crown of your head. Keep the chin in toward the chest, to avoid arching your neck. Ultimately, you should feel length from your heel to the crown of your head.

SEATED TWISTING POSTURES

The seated twisting postures provide the same benefits as the standing ones; the only difference is that there is less balance required when seated and you are grounding from your pelvis instead of your legs. If your hamstrings, hips, and spine are stiff it can be challenging to create length in the spine while twisting. Starting with a reclined version of the seated twist gives you a chance to feel the length of your spine as you practice twisting from your midback. This will help you move into deeper and more challenging twisting postures in Level 2.

Don't force the twists, let them happen naturally as you breathe. Feel the length of your spine as you inhale, and move deeper into the twist as you exhale.

If twisting makes you uncomfortable, think of making something really juicy. Remember, life is about making lemonade out of lemons, right? Within the discomfort, work on feeling more at ease without putting pressure on yourself to move into a certain place. Allow the breath to take you there. You might surprise yourself by moving further than you thought. By controlling the twists in a relaxed manner you'll be able to manage whatever is going on in your life with vitality, clarity, and a positive approach. Lemonade, anyone?

Reclined Spinal Twist

Benefit: Reclined Spinal Twist stretches the muscles along the spine independently so they can balance. The twist stimulates the nerves

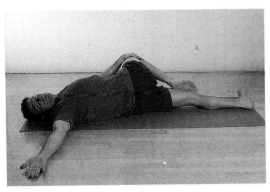

along the spine as well. It provides energy and tones the belly and the internal organs. Because it opens the chest, it improves breathing.

Reclined Spinal Twist strengthens: Quadriceps, shin, buttocks; plus core (obliques, transverse abdominis)

Reclined Spinal Twist stretches: Outer thigh, buttocks, ankle, plus middle and upper spine, core (oblique), latissimus dorsi, shoulders (anterior), biceps

Complementary strength exercises: Oblique rotation

Complementary yoga postures: Marichyasana C, Rotated triangle pose

Recline on the floor. Inhale as you draw your right knee toward your chest. Place your left hand to the outside of your right knee. Exhale as you rotate toward your left from your midback. Make sure both shoulder blades stay grounded on the floor. Gaze toward your right fingertips. Hold for 5 to 8 breath cycles. Repeat using your left side. When you have finished both sides, draw both knees to your chest and roll up to sit.

FOCUS ON FORM

Breath/Focus: Make sure you are not twisting more than will allow you to breathe fully in the twist. Keep your focus toward the fingers; make sure your neck feels comfortable.

Ground: Your foundation is your pelvis, spine, and leg. You are grounding from your pelvis to the foot, and from the pelvis to the crown of your head.

Exhale   Inhale   Exhale   Inhale   Exhale

Center: Keep your pelvis in a neutral position, even when you twist. Stack your hips and do not pull on the lower back when you rotate; make sure you feel length through your lower spine. Keep your belly engaged to avoid rocking your pelvis back and forth.

Expand: It is extremely important that you twist from your midback (the bottom of your ribs). Pay attention to this by keeping your shoulder blades grounded. Your right knee need not touch the floor. Keep your breasbone lifted, relax the shoulders, and keep the shoulder blades rolled back.

Lengthen: Make sure you maintain the length of your spine from your tailbone to the crown of your head, even when you are twisting.

BACK BENDING POSTURES

Backward bends are the opposite of forward bends. They are generally considered an active process, countering the work of gravity.

We call back bends "heart openers" and antidepressants because they expand the chest and encourage inhalation (great for asthmatics) and an attitude of embracing life. Back bends stretch the muscles of the front body (front of the neck, shoulders, chest, abdomen, hip flexors, and quadriceps). They require strength and energy to perform, but in return they increase energy, youthfulness, and vitality. In order to obtain energy, you must use energy; in this case you get it back tenfold.

Arching the spine decompresses the vertebra, and can prevent slipped discs (if you already have a slipped disc consult your physician before practicing them). It improves circulation to the lumbar spine and tones the nerves. It improves posture and the communication between the body and brain.

To prevent or ease back pain it's important to keep the musculature along the spinal column both strong and flexible. Most back pain is related to muscle imbalances, but it can also be attributed to mental tension and a stressful lifestyle. Backward bending postures can help you correct neuromuscular imbalances, but it is important to ease into them by synchronizing your movement with your breath.

Are you a person who bends over backward to please people? If you are, you might find back bends easier to do than forward bends. Continue to do the back bends but make sure you counterbalance with forward bending postures. If you have difficulty bending backward, there might be a fear of embracing what life has to offer you. In this case, also ease your way into them; as you do you'll develop more tolerance for them and you'll be able to face whatever life brings, knowing you will have both the strength and flexibility to handle it. Take care of yourself first; then you can help others.

In seated back bending postures you ground through your pelvis. It's important to:

▲ Maintain a neutral pelvic position and engage your core muscles. If there's a "crunchy" feeling in your lower back your pelvis is not positioned correctly.

▲ Expand through the rib cage by keeping your breastbone lifted, shoulders relaxed, head lifted. and shoulder blades drawn together. This encourages length in your spine; the height comes as your inhalations deepen.

Half Frog Pose

Benefits: Half Frog pose is primarily a flexibility pose, but it also gives you strength. It stretches and strengthens each side of the body independently and improves your posture by keeping the front body open and flexible and the back and spine supple and strong. This is a precursor to deeper backward bending poses. It improves circulation in the lower back region and relieves fatigue by toning the spinal nerves. This pose also helps stimulate digestion and can relieve constipation.

Half Frog pose strengthens: Biceps, trapezius, erector spinae; and bent leg: buttocks, hamstrings

Half Frog pose stretches: Core (rectus abdominis), chest, shoulder (anterior); and bent leg: quadriceps, hip flexor, shin, ankle, foot, toes

Complementary strength exercises: Single hamstring curl

Complementary yoga postures: Upward-Facing Dog pose, Locust pose, Bow pose

Lie on your belly and support yourself on your forearms in a semi-Cobra pose. Make sure your elbows are in line with your shoulders. Keep your legs together and point your toes. Bend your right leg and, with your right hand, take hold of your right ankle. If your muscles are very tight in the front of your thigh (quadriceps), this may be all that you can do initially. If you can stretch further, press your heel toward your buttocks and move your hand to the top of your foot with fingers pointing down. You might also try to rotate your hand so your fingers point toward your buttocks. Hold for 5 to 8 full breath cycles. Repeat with the left side.

FOCUS ON FORM

Breath/Focus: You should be able to breathe fully the whole time. If you cannot, you must adjust your position. Gaze at a spot in front of you while being aware of how this affects your lower and upper spine.

Ground: You are grounding through your pelvis.

Center: Draw your tailbone in to maintain a neutral pelvic position. Keep your belly active to protect your lower spine as you keep yourself lifted to get a good quadriceps stretch.

Expand: Keep the breastbone lifted and shoulders relaxed, and draw your shoulder blades into your back. Avoid sinking into your shoulders.

Lengthen: Maintain length from your tailbone to the crown of your head.

Modification

Exhale   Inhale/Exhale Inhale/Exhale Inhale/Exhale   Inhale   Exhale

Locust Pose

Benefits: Locust pose is an extension of Half Frog pose (and also a precursor to backward bending poses), and is both a strength and a flexibility pose. It improves your posture by keeping the front body open and flexible and the back and spine supple and strong. It improves circulation in the lower back region and relieves fatigue by toning the spinal nerves. This pose also helps to stimulate digestion and relieve constipation.

Locust pose strengthens: Core (transverse abdominis, erector spinae), hamstrings, buttocks, upper back (trapezius, rhomboids, latissimus dorsi), shoulders (rear), triceps

Locust pose stretches: Core (rectus abdominis), diaphragm, hip flexors, quadriceps, shins, ankles, chest, shoulders, neck (anterior)

Complementary strength exercises: Hamstring curl

Complementary yoga postures: Upward-Facing Dog pose, Half Frog pose, Bow pose

Lie face down on your stomach with your arms alongside your body with the palms facing up. Keep your legs together and your toes pointed. Look forward and focus on a spot on the floor. You should feel length in the back of your neck. Inhale and lift your chest, legs, and arms off the floor. Exhale as you reach the top of the lift. Hold the pose for 5 breath cycles. Exhale as you lower to the floor. You can repeat this two or three times.

Exhale   Inhale/Exhale   Exhale

FOCUS ON FORM

Breath/Focus: It's a little challenging at first to breathe on your stomach—this is why it's extra important that you position yourself correctly to create more space for breathing. Inhale as you lift; exhale as you lower. Gaze at a spot in front of you throughout.

Ground: You are grounding through your pelvis. Make sure you keep your pelvis in a neutral position by drawing your tailbone under and pressing your pubic bone into the floor.

Center: If your pelvis is positioned correctly, there is no need to over-squeeze the buttocks. By keeping the belly active you will protect your lower spine.

Expand: Relax your shoulders, draw your shoulder blades down and together, and keep your breastbone lifted. Feel the expansion from the bottom of your front ribs.

Lengthen: You are lengthening from your tailbone to the crown of your head. It's very important to position your body correctly. The moment your pelvis is in the correct position you'll be able to create length with the inhalation, naturally giving you more lift.

Child's Pose

Benefit: Child's pose is a flexibility pose and is very relaxing and nurturing, yet at the same time energizing. It's often used as a counter pose after backward bending poses, or sequenced between or after more challenging poses. It's a great position in which to connect with yourself.

Inhale/Exhale

Child's pose strengthens: Core (transverse abdominis)

Child's pose stretches: Ankles, shins, quadriceps, hips, spine

Complementary strength exercises: Leg press

Complementary yoga postures: Upward-Facing Dog pose, Downward-Facing Dog pose, Frog pose

From Locust pose position, inhale as you sit back onto your heels. Exhale as you fold your torso over your legs, while resting your arms at your sides and your forehead on the floor. Close your eyes and breathe for 5 to 10 breath cycles or more, if you want.

FOCUS ON FORM

Breath/Focus: Keep the breath deep and steady and breathe as if you want to puff up the back to release any tension. Eyes are closed with your gaze toward your third eye (between the eyebrows).

Ground: You are grounding through your legs (shins) to your pelvis.

Center: You center through the pelvis, but because of this restorative and gentle position your lower back is very protected.

Expand: Avoid collapsing into the pose. There should be a gentle lifting of the breastbone so the shoulders stay away from the ears.

Lengthen: You are lengthening from your tailbone to the crown of your head. Rest on your forehead.

RELAXATION

Relaxation is the "dessert" at the end of your practice. For most people it's hard to relax. The mind goes 190 miles per hour and to slow that down with the body takes some time. That's the whole idea. It's not about going faster; that just causes fatigue, injury, and exhaustion and creates wrinkles and tension. So try to carve out 5 or more minutes after your workouts and yoga practice to "take some time out."

It takes the nervous system five times longer to rejuvenate than it does tired muscles. This is why it is important to take breaks. When the nervous system is fatigued our balance and skills diminish, exercise is less fun, and we use more muscular energy than necessary. You actually become in worse shape if your exercise without rest.

Withdrawing from the external environment by calming down the overstimulated senses to draw them into the internal environment will benefit you. We'll explore this further in Levels 2 and 3. For now, relaxation will help you to pay attention to how your body is responding to the work you're doing. If you want your best body ever it's imperative. If you can't relax and feel comfortable you'll never be able to meditate, which has nothing to do with just closing the eyes. It involves full concentration on one object for a long period of time. Relaxation makes you present and will give you renewed strength.

The physical yoga practice will help release tensions and tightness so you'll eventually be comfortable in these positions for longer periods of time. What's most important is that you take the time and that you relax as much as you can. It really will make you feel refreshed.

The more you do it, the more space you create in your life. Remember, we create space and we create time. It's about the choices we make. Make choices for yourself that will give you energy, not drain you. Life is too short. The relaxation posture for Level 1 is called Savasana (final relaxation pose).

Final Relaxation Pose (Savasana)

Lie on the floor on your back and close your eyes and mouth. Open your legs about shoulder-width apart, and let your feet naturally flip to the side. Keep your arms at your sides with your palms facing up. Lift your buttocks so you can adjust your lower back. Adjust your shoulders so both of your shoulder

blades relax evenly on the floor. Keep your chin drawn toward your chest, so the back of your neck is long. If you find your neck arches too much, fold a towel and place it behind your head for support to ease tight neck muscles. If your lower back feels uncomfortable, roll a blanket or a towel and put it behind your knees to give extra support to your back. Put on extra clothes or a comfy blanket to ensure that you stay warm; it's hard to relax when you are cold.

Practice free breathing and allow your breath to expand your belly on the inhale; let the belly go back to normal on the exhale. See how long you can stay focused on your breath before your mind gets distracted. Whatever distractions come your way, think about it for as long as you must and then try to work your mind back into your breath again. This teaches you to be present in the moment.

Light a candle, burn incense, massage your temples or neck with lavender oil, or use a lavender-infused eye pillow—anything that will help to adjust your body and mind into a state of relaxation.

Strength Training—Body Weight

LOWER BODY

Leg strength is the foundation for all sports and aids in everyday life movements as well.

If your legs and buttock muscles lack strength, a lot of stress is put on your joints over time, which can result in low back, hip, knee, and ankle injuries. Lack of lower body strength also creates unnecessary strain on the upper body.

The leg exercises learned in Level 1 lay the foundation for overall leg strength and stability. Get to know these leg exercises using your own body weight to focus on good form (alignment) and to make sure you are doing them correctly before you start to work out with free weights.

You must do these basic leg exercises with good form to be able to progress to Levels 2 and 3. All these exercises contribute to increasing your leg strength, and develop both tone and shape in your lower body muscles. These exercises will also complement the standing yoga postures.

Get your best leg up!

BODY WEIGHT

Squat

The squat is designed to develop tone, definition, and strength in your lower body. It also challenges balance, coordination, and full body integration. It's one of the most effective exercises to shape the lower body. It is very important to do the squat correctly; otherwise, it can be harmful for the lower back and knees. Get to know the squat with your own body weight to work on alignment and make sure you are doing it correctly before you add on free weights.

The squat strengthens and stretches: Quadriceps, buttocks, hamstrings, shins, core (transverse abdominis, erector spinae)

Complementary strength poses: Balancing on both feet

Complementary flexibility poses: Reclined Extended hand to big toe pose, Frog pose

Stand with your legs hip-width apart, arms at your side. Engage your quadriceps and belly. Keep shoulders relaxed, breastbone lifted, and focus on a spot in front of you. Inhale, bend at the knees and hips, and lean back into your heels as if you're going to sit into a chair. Extend your arms to shoulder height in front of you. Exhale as you return to starting position. Do 12 to 20 repetitions.

FOCUS ON FORM

Breath/Focus: Connect the breath with the movement for full breaths. Inhale as you lower; exhale as you lift. Gaze in front of you as you breathe and pay attention to how your body is reacting to the squat.

Ground: You are grounding from the feet to the pelvis. Keep toes spread and slightly lifted so you lean into your heels, taking the pressure off your knees. Do not lower beyond a 90-degree angle.

Center: Keep your belly engaged to provide protection for your lower back.

Expand: Keep your breastbone lifted and shoulders relaxed so you can fully inhale when you lower into the squat and fully exhale as you lift.

Lengthen: You are lengthening from your pelvis to the crown of your head. Think of being a connected unit so you avoid moving the torso independently from the legs. Imagine balancing a book on the crown of your head, and as you move, make sure the book doesn't fall off. This will help maintain length in your spine the whole time (without straining your neck).

Exhale   Inhale   Exhale

Lunge

Benefit: The lunge is designed to tone, define, and strengthen the muscles in the lower body. It also challenges your balance, coordination, and full body integration. Just like the squat, proper alignment is essential for good results. Learning the lunge using just your body weight will help you achieve your best form when you add external weight.

The lunge strengthens and stretches: Quadriceps, buttocks, hamstrings, shins, belly (rectus abdominis), erector spinae

Complementary strength poses: Standing postures and in particular, Tree pose

Complementary flexibility poses: Reclined Extended Hand to Big Toe pose, Frog pose

Stand with your legs hip-width apart, arms at your side. Engage your quadriceps and belly. Keep your shoulders relaxed, your breastbone lifted, and your focus on a spot in front of you. Step your right leg back into a lunge position. Make sure your left knee is parallel with your ankle and keep your right leg slightly bent. From this position, inhale, lower your right knee toward the floor, and exhale as you lift. Make sure your left knee doesn't move back and forth. Do 12 to 20 repetitions on this leg, return to starting position, and repeat on the other leg.

FOCUS ON FORM

Breath/Focus: Keep breathing full breath cycles as you are executing the movements. Inhale as you lower, exhale as you lift. Gaze at a spot

Exhale   Inhale

in front of you while being aware of how your body is responding to the lunge, and adjust accordingly throughout.

Ground: You are grounding from your feet. At first, the movement might feel like there is more weight on your front leg than your back leg; over time as you work with the centering, expanding, and lengthening aspects of the lunge you will transfer weight into the back leg and you will feel more balanced.

Center: Draw your tailbone under and engage the belly muscles to create stability and protection for the lower back, and to gain better control over your torso.

Expand: Keep your breastbone lifted, and shoulders relaxed, and draw the shoulder blades together into your back. This creates lightness and space in your torso for your breath to give you support to perform the lunge.

Lengthen: You are lengthening from your pelvis to the crown of your head. It's important to keep your torso as vertical as possible, and to avoid leaning your torso over your front leg. Trust that your legs are strong enough to support you, and they will. When they're tired, end the set, and continue next time. Don't sacrifice good form!

The Bridge Support

Benefit: The bridge support is designed to build strength, tone, and stability in your lower body muscles but also increase your balance, coordination, and full body integration.

Muscles that are being strengthened (the same muscles need stretching): Buttocks, hamstrings, shins, core (transverse abdominis), upper back (trapezius, rhomboids), erector spinae

Complementary strength poses: Back-bending poses, Locust pose

Complementary flexibility poses: Reclined Extended Hand to Big Toe pose, Half Frog pose

Lie on your back, arms at your sides. Bend your legs, keeping your feet grounded on the floor, hip-width apart. Keep the back of your neck long. Focus on a spot on the ceiling. Press your feet against the floor. Inhale as you lift your pelvis toward the ceiling. Contract your buttocks and hamstrings. Exhale at the top of the lift. Try to hold this bridge position for 5 to 10 breath cycles. Exhale as you slowly roll down, vertebra by vertebra, to starting position. Inhale as you lift; exhale as you lower. Repeat 10 times.

When you feel stable in the bridge position, move on to single leg support. Place a block between your knees and inhale as you lift back into bridge pose. Engaging your inner thighs and squeezing your knees together, exhale as you extend your right leg. (If you slant too much in your pelvis or feel any strain in your neck, practice the bridge pose a while longer before taking on the single leg bridge.) Hold the pose for 5 to 10 breath cycles. Inhale. Lower the leg to bridge pose and exhale rolling down vertebra by vertebra to the starting position. Inhale as you lift. Exhale as you extend your leg. Inhale as you bend your leg. Exhale as you lower to the floor. Repeat with the left leg.

FOCUS ON FORM

Breath/Focus: If you find it challenging to connect the breath with the movement, at least make sure to avoid holding your breath. Keep your gaze at the ceiling the whole time; focus your awareness of how your body is responding and adjust accordingly.

Ground: You are grounding from your feet, but also through your upper back. Although you can't see your feet directly, make sure they remain parallel the whole time.

Center: Use your hands to feel the positioning of your pelvis. Make sure your hips don't drop or become uneven. This may happen if one

Exhale   Inhale   Exhale   Inhale   Exhale

leg is weaker than the other. Only lift as high as you can and maintain proper alignment. Position the pelvis into a neutral position and engage your belly. Think about the way you position your pelvis in the back-bending poses, and apply that to this exercise.

Expand: Lift the breast bone toward the chin, relax the shoulders, and draw the shoulder blades together while keeping your arms shoulder-width apart.

Lengthen: You are lengthening from your tailbone to the crown of your head. By applying and practicing the grounding, centering, and expanding principles, you will get the support your spine needs to lengthen.

MACHINES

Leg Press

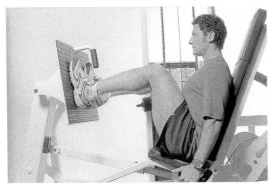

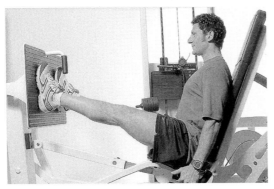

Benefit: The leg press is designed to build strength, tone, and stability in your lower body muscles.

There are different types of leg press machines. Try to alternate between the kind where you push the weight away from you and the type where you push your body away from the weight. If you don't have access to a leg press machine, you can do squats and lunges that complement the leg press.

Muscles being strengthened and stretched: Buttocks, quadriceps, hamstrings, calves

Assisting muscles: Belly (transverse abdominis)

Complementary strength poses: Standing postures, Attention pose, Tree pose

Complementary flexibility poses: Reclined Extended Hand to Big Toe pose, Half Frog pose

Choose your weight and adjust the back pad to allow for comfort and full range of motion. Lean back and rest your back and head on the back pad. Position both legs on the board about hip-width apart, with feet parallel. Hold onto the handles. Exhale as you extend your legs by pressing your feet against the plate (more from your heels than your forefoot). Inhale as you return to the starting position by bending your legs, and drawing your knees toward your chest. Do 15 to 20 repetitions.

FOCUS ON FORM

Breath/Focus: Keep your focus in front of you. Breath should be full and deep to match the intense work of the leg press. Exhale as you extend the legs. Inhale as you bend the legs.

Ground: You are grounded through your pelvis and feet. Your upper body is stationary, which gives you a great advantage, allowing you to put some force behind your leg muscles. Make sure you contract your quadriceps as you extend your leg, and press from your heels. Avoid hyperextending your knees as you extend your legs.

Center: Position the pelvis so your lower back is protected. Engage the press from the belly.

Expand: Keep the breastbone lifted, shoulders relaxed, and shoulder blades drawn together. Rest your head back so you're not straining your neck muscles.

Lengthen: You are lengthening through your spine. Make sure that even if your spine is supported by the back pad the weight you have chosen doesn't cause too much pressure on the lower spine.

Inhale   Exhale

TORSO

You know we don't do "abdominal work" anymore, right? It's all about doing core work and developing core strength.

The difference between abdominal work and core work is that core work is all about integrating the full torso in any work you do. When doing biceps curls, you make sure your entire core is supporting you. Whether you are doing squats, lunges, or the triangle posture—the core is with you in any possible direction. If your core is strong and flexible it will help you balance better and give you more energy.

Everyone wants to do the "fancy" core work exercises, but they're difficult to master, and it takes the ability to isolate the core muscles throughout the exercise, which is not easy to do! Although the basic crunch and the basic oblique rotation are not considered "core exercises" I consider them "core" to the Goa System. These muscles assist in breathing and help complement all the categories of yoga postures. Yes, they are basic and they work the superficial muscles, but they are the foundation for all the core exercises. You have to start somewhere, and these two exercises are a great way to help you isolate and feel your muscles, while connecting your breath with the movement. This way you can work more intensely into those deep core muscles.

Most people perform these exercises the wrong way. No matter how basic something is, if you can't do it, or if you're not doing it correctly, then you'll never be able to move deeper into the next level.

It's important to be able to isolate the area you want to work, find your correct range of motion, and link the breath with the movement. When you can do that without straining your breath or your neck muscles, you can move on to the Level 2 stability ball exercises.

Basic Crunch

Benefit: The basic crunch is designed to isolate your belly muscles (especially the rectus and transverse abdominis). It also teaches you to connect the breath with the movement. Although this is called a basic crunch it's the most important one to do correctly, since it's the foundation for all of the rest of the core work we do in the Goa System.

Muscles being strengthened and stretched: Rectus abdominis, transverse abdominis

Complementary strength poses: Plank pose, Chaturanga

Complementary flexibility poses: Backward bends such as Upward-Facing Dog

Lie on the floor with your legs bent, hip-width apart and feet grounded, fingers (unclasped) behind your head, and elbows pointing out to the side. Focus forward toward the ceiling. Exhale as you roll your upper back (bottom of the shoulder blades) off the floor—go no further. As you lift, make sure you contract your lower belly muscles by pulling your navel in toward your spine. Initiate the movement from your belly. Inhale as you lower toward the floor again. Do not lower all the way to the floor, only three-quarters of the way down. Your shoulders should be relaxed. If you feel any strain in your neck, you are working too much from the neck; engage the belly more and relax the neck. Do 15 to 20 repetitions.

FOCUS ON FORM

Breath/Focus: Keep the focus in front of you toward the ceiling the whole time; make sure your breath is smooth while you execute the movement. If the breath is strained, work with the exercise until the breath smoothes out. Exhale as you lift; inhale as you lower.

Ground: You are grounding through your spine and feet.

Center: Draw your tailbone under slightly so that you keep your pelvis in a neutral position and engage your belly muscles. Make sure the lower spine is protected on the floor.

Inhale   Exhale   Inhale

Expand: Although you are rounding forward slightly, do not pull on the neck muscle and crunch through the heart to execute the lift. Keep the breastbone lifted so that the shoulders and neck relax. This will allow you to create more space in the rib cage so that you can do the work and breathe at the same time.

Lengthen: You are still lengthening from the tailbone to the crown of your head.

Basic Oblique Rotation

Benefit: The Basic Oblique is designed to strengthen and tone your waistline. It also teaches you to rotate from the midback without straining and pulling on your lower back or neck muscles. Although it's called a basic oblique rotation it is vital that you do it correctly because, like the basic crunch, it is the foundation for all of the rest of the core work we do in the Goa System.

Muscles being strengthened and stretched: External and internal obliques

Complementary strength poses: Standing side lateral bends such as Triangle pose; twists such as Reverse Triangle pose, and Reclined Extended Hand to Big Toe pose

Complementary flexibility poses: Standing side lateral bends such as Triangle pose; twists such as Revolved Triangle pose, and Reclined Extended Hand to Big Toe pose

Inhale   Exhale   Inhale

Lie on the floor with your legs bent and hip-width apart, feet grounded with your fingers (unclasped) behind your head and your elbows pointing out to the side. Focus forward toward the ceiling. Place your right ankle over your left knee. Exhale as you rotate your left shoulder toward your right knee. As you rotate, make sure to keep your hip bones anchored to the floor so that your pelvis is stable, allowing you to rotate from your midback (from the bottom of your ribs). Your elbows should point out the whole time. Inhale as you rotate back to the center. Do 15 to 20 repetitions.

FOCUS ON FORM

Breath/Focus: Your point of focus changes as you rotate, but keep it in front of you the whole time and make sure your breath is smooth and even during the movement. If the breath is strained, work with the exercise until it smoothes out. Exhale as you cross, inhale as you come back to center.

Ground: You are grounding through your spine and feet.

Center: Draw your tailbone under slightly to keep your pelvis in a neutral position, allowing you to fully engage the belly muscles; make sure the lower spine is protected on the floor.

Expand: Although you are rounding forward slightly, do not pull on the neck muscle and crunch through the heart to execute the rotation. As you rotate, make sure you rotate from the bottom of your ribs and rotate as a unit. Keep the breastbone lifted so that your shoulders and neck relax. This will create more space in the rib cage, allowing you to do the work and breathe at the same time.

Lengthen: You are still lengthening from the tailbone to the crown of your head.

CHEST

The chest and back muscles are interdependent, so it's important to keep both strong.

The chest exercise presented here incorporates exercise tubing; this helps you isolate the chest muscles and increase their strength. It will also lift and improve the overall appearance of your chest.

In order to execute a Chaturanga you need chest support, and with stronger chest muscles you'll be able to hold the arm balancing positions longer, while being able to breathe fully.

You want to make sure you balance the strength and flexibility of your chest muscles, otherwise your posture may be affected with rounded shoulders (tight chest muscles) or a hunched back (overstretched back muscles). If your chest muscles are tight your upper back muscles are overstretched. This results in rounded shoulders, a hunched back, and poor posture. In this case, be sure you stretch your chest muscles with back-bending postures and strengthen your upper back muscles by using resistance (in this case, tubing).

Tubing

Tubing comes in different resistances according to color. Check the resource guide for more information.

Standing Chest Press

Benefit: The standing chest press increases strength and tone in the chest muscles. It also teaches full body integration, stabilization, and balance.

Muscles being strengthened and stretched: Chest, serratus anterior

Assisting muscles: Triceps, shoulders (anterior), core (transverse abdominis), erector spinae, quadriceps, buttocks, hamstrings, shins, ankles, feet

Complementary strength poses: Plank pose, Chaturanga

Complementary flexibility poses: Locust pose, Bow pose

Inhale   Exhale   Inhale

If you don't have a partner to work with then tie the tubing to a fixed, stable, stationary object such as a pole, a doorknob, or a piece of gym equipment. Stand with your legs hip-width apart (or shoulder-width apart if you have trouble balancing), and your feet parallel. Grasp the handles of the tubing apparatus with your palm facing down. Bring the tubing under your armpits, to shoulder height. Keep your knees bent and your pelvis in a neutral position with your belly engaged and your rib cage lifted.

Exhale as you extend your arms without locking your elbows. Inhale as you bend your arms while maintaining a 90-degree angle. Keep your wrists straight. Avoid using too hard a grip. Do 12 to 20 repetitions.

FOCUS ON FORM

Breath/Focus: Exhale as you extend your arms; inhale as you bend. Gaze at a point in front of you while being aware of your body posture while moving your arm.

Ground: You are grounding from your feet. Make sure to keep your knees slightly bent.

Center: Keep your pelvis in a neutral position. The belly must be fully engaged to maintain support for your lower spine.

Expand: Keep your rib cage fully lifted by lifting the breastbone. Relax your shoulders and you'll be able to more fully isolate the chest muscles and breathe.

Lengthen: You are lengthening from your tailbone to the crown of your head. Make sure, regardless of the amount of resistance you use, that you center and expand yourself in order to maintain length in your spine.

BACK

The back and chest muscles are interdependent, so it's important to keep both strong. A strong back is also critical to good performance in most sports.

The back exercise presented here will help you isolate and strengthen your upper and middle back. Most people's upper back muscles are over-stretched. Because of hunching, the shoulder blades slide forward and away from the spine and the trapezius muscles progressively grow weaker. This lack of upper back strength promotes poor posture.

You now know the side effects of poor posture—poor energy flow, fatigue, and depression; and you can't possibly look your best with poor posture. This back-strengthening exercise will complement the extension you need in your spine to practice all of the yoga postures. This will increase awareness of your posture and motivate you to build a better body.

Your best body stands tall!

TUBING

Standing Row

Benefit: The standing row is designed to increase strength and tone the upper back muscles. It also teaches full body integration, stabilization, and balance.

Muscles being strengthened and stretched: Rhomboids, trapezius, latissimus dorsi, teres major, shoulder (posterior)

Assisting: Biceps, belly (transverse abdominis), erector spinae, quadriceps, buttocks, hamstrings, shins, ankles, feet

Complementary strength poses: Downward-Facing Dog pose, Upward-Facing Dog pose

Complementary flexibility poses: Triangle pose, Reverse Triangle pose

Inhale   Exhale   Inhale

If you don't have a partner to work with then tie tubing to a fixed object that is both stable and stationary such as a pole, a doorknob, or a piece of gym equipment. Stand with your legs hip-width apart (or shoulder-width apart if you have trouble balancing), and your feet should be parallel. Grasp the handles with your palms facing each other. Start with your arms extended at shoulder height, making sure there is resistance from the tubing. Keep your knees bent and your pelvis in a neutral position with the belly fully engaged and the rib cage lifted. Keep your elbows close to the body as you exhale and pull your elbows back while contracting your shoulder blades together. Inhale as you extend your arms. Keep your wrists straight and avoid using too hard a grip. Do 12 to 20 repetitions.

FOCUS ON FORM

Breath/Focus: Exhale as you bend your arms; inhale as you extend. Gaze at a point in front of you while being aware of your body posture through the arm movement.

Ground: You are grounding from your feet. Make sure to keep your knees slightly bent.

Center: Keep your pelvis in a neutral position. The belly must be fully engaged to maintain support for your lower spine.

Expand: Keep your rib cage lifted by lifting your breastbone. Relax your shoulders to better isolate your upper back muscles and breathe more fully.

Lengthen: You are lengthening from your tailbone to the crown of your head. Make sure that regardless of the amount of resistance you use you center and expand yourself in order to maintain length in your spine.

BICEPS

The biceps is the muscle on the front upper arm. You are going to isolate and increase your biceps strength with exercise tubing and the standing biceps curl. This exercise will strengthen and give support to your shoulder, elbow, and wrist. Make sure you don't over-grip the handles on the tubing. It is enough to cup your hand around the handle. Be sure to keep your wrists even and not bent.

Remember; although you are working individual muscle groups here, you are still working your body as a connected unit.

This biceps work helps provide strength and support in your elbows, wrists, fingers, and hands for the arm balancing postures.

TUBING

Standing Biceps Curl

Benefit: The standing biceps curl is designed to increase strength and tone in the front of the arm (the biceps muscles). It also teaches full body integration, stabilization, and balance.

Muscles being strengthened and stretched: Biceps

Assisting muscles: Upper back muscles, core (transverse abdominis), erector spinae, quadriceps, buttocks, hamstrings, shins, ankles, feet

Complementary strength poses: Downward-Facing Dog pose, Plank pose, Chaturanga

Complementary flexibility poses: Bow pose, reclined spinal twist

Hold the handles as you step on the tubing with your right foot, keeping the left leg behind you and legs hip-width apart. (Both legs are slightly bent). Position the pelvis, engage the belly, and lift the rib cage. Keep the palms facing forward and the elbows close to the body the whole time. Exhale as you bend your lower arm and inhale as you extend. Keep your wrists straight and avoid gripping the handles too hard. Do 12 to 20 repetitions.

Inhale   Exhale   Inhale

Breath/Focus: Exhale as you bend your arms; inhale as you extend. Gaze at a point in front of you while being aware of your body posture through the arm movement.

Ground: You are grounding from your feet. Keep your knees slightly bent.

Center: Keep your pelvis in a neutral position. The belly must be fully engaged to maintain support for your lower spine and to avoid hunching your upper spine.

Expand: Keep your rib cage lifted by lifting the breastbone. Relax your shoulders to better isolate your biceps muscles and breathe more fully.

Lengthen: You are lengthening from your tailbone to the crown of your head. Make sure that regardless of the amount of resistance you use you center and expand yourself in order to maintain length in your spine.

TRICEPS

The triceps is the muscle on the back upper arm; this is a problem area for many people. Like the previous biceps exercise, the triceps will be worked with exercise tubing. This will tone and increase the strength of your triceps muscles and strengthen and give support to your shoulders, elbows, and wrists.

You need to use a tighter grip than with the biceps curl, but make sure you don't overgrip, and keep your wrists even and not bent. Remember; although you are working individual muscle groups here, you are still working your body as a connected unit.

This triceps work will complement the need for strength and support in your elbows, wrists, fingers, and hands for the arm balancing postures, such as the Plank pose and the yoga push-up, Chaturanga.

Tubing Standing Triceps Kickback

Benefit: The standing triceps kickback is designed to increase strength and tone in the back of the arm (the triceps muscles). It also teaches full body integration, stabilization, and balance.

Muscles being strengthened and stretched: Triceps

Assisting: Upper back muscles, core (transverse abdominis, erector spinae), quadriceps, buttocks, hamstrings, shins, ankles, feet

Complementary strength poses: Upward-Facing Dog pose

Complementary flexibility poses: Downward-Facing Dog pose

Hold one handle with your right hand as you step on the tubing with your left foot and step your right foot backward into a lunge position, keeping your legs hip-width apart. Gain support by placing your left hand on your left thigh. Keep the palm of your right hand facing backward as you lift your right elbow to shoulder height. Exhale as you extend your lower arm and inhale as you bend. Adjust the tubing according to the resistance you need to execute the movement. The only part of your body that moves is your right lower arm. Keep your elbow at shoulder height the whole time. Keep your wrists straight and avoid gripping the handle too hard. Do 12 to 20 repetitions. Repeat on the other side.

FOCUS ON FORM

Breath/Focus: Exhale as you extend your arm; inhale as you bend. Gaze toward the floor while being aware of your body posture through the arm movement.

Inhale   Exhale   Inhale

Ground: You are grounding from your feet. Make sure to transfer the weight onto the back leg to avoid overworking the front leg muscles.

Center: Keep your pelvis as neutral as possible. Draw your tailbone under and keep your belly fully engaged to maintain support for your lower spine.

Expand: Keep your rib cage lifted by lifting the breastbone. Relax your shoulders to better isolate your triceps muscles and breathe fully.

Lengthen: You are lengthening from your tailbone to the crown of your head. Make sure that regardless of how much resistance you use you center and expand yourself in order to maintain length in your spine.

Level 1 Endurance

This walking program can be performed outdoors or indoors using a treadmill. The power of walking is often underestimated. It's a very low impact activity and involves the entire body. Remember, running is just an extension of walking. It's the same movement; running is simply a higher-impact exercise. The better you walk, the more efficiently you will run. If running is not comfortable for you, power walking is a great alternative. In Level 1, we start with walking.

Walking doesn't take much skill. You can do it anywhere you are. It takes higher intensity, however, to create a high heart rate when walking as compared to running. Many walkers begin developing bad form when they try to increase their intensity and use a lot of arm movements, which causes a great deal of strain on the shoulders and especially the rotator cuffs. Adding on hand weights will not help.

If you walk outside be sure to vary the terrain. If you walk on a treadmill, add some hill training.

Supportive Conditioning Exercises

The following often get overtaxed and need flexibility practice:

Feet (soreness, tight plantar arches), ankles, calves, hamstrings, inner thighs, buttocks, hip flexors, spine/lower back, shoulders, neck. The muscles that are often underutilized and need strength are:

Upper back muscles (trapezius, rhomboids), arms (biceps/triceps), shoulders (rotator cuffs), and core muscles (abdominals/lower back).

Walking Posture and Technique

Your body is your tool when you power walk, so it's important you match your body posture to your walking technique. The posture in walking is erect, but dynamic. The yoga categories most applicable for walking/running are those involved in the standing balancing poses. You are grounding through your feet, centering through your pelvis and core, lengthening through your spine, and expanding through your rib cage.

If your upper back muscles are too flexible and the chest muscles too tight, your body may hunch and your shoulders tighten, which will inhibit your breathing. All of this will have a negative effect on the lower back and hamstrings as well.

The stronger your upper body is, the more your legs can work. A combination of strength and flexibility in your legs is going to help your upper body relax more and elongate better. A strong core connecting the upper body and lower body will allow them to work together in unison.

Lower Body

It's important to walk with light steps—not that you are trying to tiptoe, but trying to create lightness in your body. This will put more spring in your step and will decrease the pressure on your joints. If you "stomp" you are actually working less efficiently; all that stomping does nothing to increase the intensity of your aerobic workout.

It's important you use your whole foot by rolling from your heel to the forefoot to the toes so that you hit the pavement evenly. As you leave the ground, give a little push with your big toe.

To get more bounce and lightness in your walk, try to flex your ankles, which will stretch and strengthen them. The less rigid they are, the more lightness you can create. Practicing the yoga postures recommended in Level 1 will stretch and strengthen your ankles.

Never lock your knees; always keep them slightly bent while walking.

Upper Body

Your goal is to lengthen from your tailbone (pelvis) to the crown of your head. Your spine must be perpendicular to the ground. Keeping your posture erect will free your legs to do their work, and you'll create more room in your torso for deep breathing.

Because of the constant forward motion in walking, the hamstrings and hip flexors get very tight. This can pull on the lower back muscles, causing the pelvis to tilt forward (anterior tilt), and resulting in a swayback.

A swayback makes it difficult to create length in your spine and inhibits the flow of energy. As you develop strength and flexibility in your core you will become more aware of your pelvis so you can better connect the upper and lower body, enabling it to move as a connected unit. As your awareness level grows, you will recognize when your core moves out of alignment. A flexible core allows the pelvis room to move with your stride and helps avoid a tendency to lock into a certain position. Stay aware of how your pelvis is responding and adjust the intensity of your workout to allow for correct positioning.

The Warm-Up

Do Sun Salutation A as the first part of your warm-up. This Sun Salutation is very helpful because it's a great counter pose. It strengthens the underutilized muscles in your upper body and stretches the overtaxed muscles in your lower body.

Moving from Chaturanga to Upward-Facing Dog and to Downward-Facing Dog will not only both stretch and strengthen your lower leg (the calf and the shins) and prevent shin splints, but will also increase circulation to the feet. Doing two rounds of the Sun Salutation A will take about $2 \frac{1}{2}$ minutes, which leaves you another $2 \frac{1}{2}$ minutes for the rest of your warm-up.

Focus

It's important to keep your focus at a spot in front of you while walking. You must be aware of where you're walking and at the same time, pay attention to how your body is responding to the workout. If you are walking outside, you also need to pay attention to where you are walking, bumps or holes in the road, the people around you, and the direction in which you are moving.

If you are walking on a treadmill try to avoid reading or watching television; rather, focus on your breath and how your body is reacting to the intensity of your movement so you can adjust accordingly. You will work more effectively and efficiently if you focus on your entire body during your workout. This also allows you to feel refreshed and energized instead of letting distractions pull your focus out of your body while moving it.

4 Week Power Walking Program

WEEK	PROGRAM	MINUTES	INTENSITY
1	Warm-up phase	3–5	40–50 %
	Target heart rate phase: flat	20	50–60 %
	Warm-down phase	3–5	Resting heart rate + 10 points
2	Warm-up phase	3–5	40–50 %
	Target heart rate phase: flat/hill	20	50–65 %
	Warm-down phase	3–5	Resting heart rate + 10 points
3	Warm-up phase	3–5	40–50 %
	Target heart rate phase: flat/very hilly/flat	20	50–60 %
	Warm-down phase	3–5	Resting heart rate + 10 points
4	Warm-up phase	3–5	40–50 %
	Target heart rate phase: flat/hilly/very hilly/flat	20	50–60 %
	Warm-down phase	3–5	Resting heart rate + 10 points

Flow and Energy

Naturally you "flow" when you power walk, so it's important to connect your breathing with the movement and intensity of your workout. Adding a supportive breath component increases the energy flow throughout your body. In fact, it is the very act of connecting the breath with the movement that creates the "flow."

Remember to calculate your working heart rate, as you learned in Chapter 2 and be sure to check your heart rate every 10 minutes to make sure you are working in your training zone. Remember to breathe with the movement; feel your heart working and the blood flowing through your body.

The Warm-Down

To begin the warm-down at the end of a walking session, slow down your pace for the last 3 minutes. As the second part of your warm-down, try the Level 1 seated forward bending, backward bending, and twisting yoga postures. These postures will help counterbalance the muscles used in all levels of walking, particularly power walking.

The core exercises in the Level 1 strength-training section will give you both strength and flexibility in your core and will help you control your arm and leg movements. This core work is essential for protecting your lower back during any form of exercise.

The upper body strength-training exercises strengthen the under-utilized muscle groups in this area, allowing you to become stronger while improving your aerobic endurance.

Safety, Caution, and Rest

Remember that your body is your tool, so when your body gets tired it needs to repair itself. After you've warmed-down and counterbalanced, it's important to rest and rejuvenate. But it's also important that you cross-train with other aerobic endurance activities so you engage and impact your muscles in different ways. Moving toward *your* best body ever!

EXERCISE SELECTION: BIKING

Biking is a low-impact, high-intensity activity. This biking program can be performed indoors or outdoors. There are different indoor bikes: recumbent bikes and upright bikes. Outdoor bikes come in one of three types—speed bikes, mountain bikes, and hybrid bikes. The choice depends on your preference and exercise location.

Outside biking demands more balance and core strength than inside biking does, because of its dynamic and ever-changing nature. In biking, the legs move dynamically and the upper body is static. Because of the forward movement (unless it's a recumbent bike) there is a lot of pressure on the upper back, shoulders, and neck, making these areas susceptible to stress and strain.

Supportive Conditioning Exercises

These muscles needed for biking often get overtaxed and need increased flexibility: chest, front shoulders, upper spine, neck (in constant flexion), hip flexors, quadriceps, calves, hamstrings

These muscles needed for biking are often underutilized and need strengthening: upper back muscles (trapezius, rhomboids), lower back, core, hamstrings, arms

Biking Posture and Technique

When you add a bike to your workout, you are adding another tool. It's important to fit one tool, your physical body, to your other tool, your bike, by finding your best body posture.

The yoga postures that are most complementary for biking are the forward bending postures. The muscles used in these postures mimic the position of your body on the bike seat. You are both grounding and centering through your pelvis (if you stand up, you're grounding through your legs), expanding through your ribcage, and lengthening through your spine.

Lower Body

Biking is low impact for the feet, but high intensity for the legs; the legs are moving and there is a push-pull action in your leg muscles. Your hips, thighs, knees, and ankles all need to be in alignment. They should not flare to the side—this signals that one side of the body is working less than the other. By keeping the hips, thighs, knees, and ankles in alignment and the muscles around them strong and flexible, you can avoid wearing down ligaments and tendons and creating imbalanced muscle groups.

Core

You are grounding from the pelvis when you're pedaling seated on the seat, and grounding through your legs when you are pedaling standing. So the principles for standing postures and forward bending postures (both standing and seated) apply here. Regardless of grounding through your pelvis, you are lengthening through your spine.

You learned in the Level 1 yoga section that there is a difference between hunching and leaning forward. Your spine must be lengthened as you lean forward over the handlebars. A hunched spine results in decreased circulation in your shoulders and neck and restricts your breathing. It is important to feel the length from your tailbone to the crown of your head.

Because you are stationary yet moving, it's easy to get sloppy with posture. You want to avoid rocking from side to side; this signals that one hip is weak or inflexible. Hips are the core of the movement for a biker. If this core is weak, the upper body must work harder, which can lead to back strain.

Although your hips are stable while on the bike they do need room to move. The way you position the saddle is important. Keep the seat almost with a tilt of only 3 to 5 degrees. This positioning allows your pelvis to move a bit while creating pelvic stability, spinal length, and energy flow throughout the body, starting in the legs and moving through the core to the crown of the head.

Upper Body

The upper body must be engaged, yet relaxed. The more tense it is, the more drained you will feel. Make adjustments as you go along. Being comfortable on the bike seat is just an adjustment away! Your spine should be lengthened as it is in a forward bend; allow the spine to use its natural curves.

Lifting the rib cage out of your hips to create space is important because it affects how the rest of your spine is going to feel. Anytime you tilt the pelvis too much during a forward bend, it affects your lower back and stretches it, which is not the goal here. This can also add too much pressure on the hands, wrists, and lower back.

Keep the front body open so the heart and lungs can breathe. Breathe deeply to take in oxygen and distribute it to your working muscles. The tighter your hamstrings are, the harder it is to get length through your spine, so you have to spend some time stretching them.

Correct positioning on the bike means that your shoulder blades are down and slightly together. There should be adequate space between your ears and your shoulders, as in the Downward-Facing Dog pose and the Upward-Facing Dog pose.

4 Week Biking Program

WEEK	PROGRAM	MINUTES	INTENSITY
1	Warm-up phase	3–5	40–50 %
	Target heart rate phase: flat	15–20	50–60 %
	Warm-down phase	3–5	Resting heart rate + 10 points
2	Warm-up phase	3–5	40–50 %
	Target heart rate phase: flat/hill	20	50–60 %
	Warm-down phase	3–5	Resting heart rate + 10 points
3	Warm-up phase	3–5	40–50 %
	Target heart rate phase: flat/very hilly/flat	20	50–60 %
	Warm-down phase	3–5	Resting heart rate + 10 points
4	Warm-up phase	3–5	40–50 %
	Target heart rate phase: flat/hilly/very hilly/flat	20	50–60 %
	Warm-down phase	3–5	Resting heart rate + 10 points

Keep your arms placed at right angles to your torso, in line with your shoulders. Your wrists must be in line with your shoulders. Don't keep your arms too far apart (think Downward-Facing Dog, Upward-Facing Dog). Holding your arms too far apart puts too much pressure on the shoulders.

Avoid dropping your head. The best positioning of the head is to keep it lifted so you maintain length in your neck. This also makes it easy see where you are going when biking outside.

The Warm-Up

Do Sun Salutation A as the first part of your warm-up. This Sun Salutation is very helpful because it's a great counter pose to your biking posture. It strengthens the underutilized muscles and stretches the overemphasized muscles.

Moving from Chaturanga to Upward-Facing Dog stretches the muscles in the front body (shoulders, chest, abdomen, shins, ankles, tops of the feet). Moving to Downward-Facing Dog stretches the hamstrings, calves, ankles, and feet, and strengthens the upper back muscles.

Doing two rounds of Sun Salutation A will take about 2 $^1/_2$ minutes, which leaves you another 2 $^1/_2$ minutes for the rest of your warm-up.

The Warm-Down

At the end of your biking session, slow down your pace for the last 3 to 5 minutes.

As the second part of your warm-down, counterbalance with the yoga twisting poses and back-bending poses.

Also do the Level 1 core yoga exercises, which will give you both strength and flexibility in your core so you will be able to balance and control the movements (or lack thereof) of the upper body and lower body. Core strength is essential in preventing overstrain of the lower back.

Focus

Your eyes should be focused forward toward the ground, but you should also be aware of how the rest of your body is reacting to the work you are doing.

If you are biking outside, your awareness level will naturally be elevated because you must pay attention to the outside environment. If you are biking inside, you may have to fine-tune your awareness to keep it activated and focused on what your body is doing. Try to avoid reading or watching television; rather, focus on your breath and how your body is reacting to the intensity of your workout in order for you to adjust accordingly. This should become a mind/body experience, leaving you feeling refreshed and energized. Your awareness can change the quality of your workout.

Flow and Energy

Because you are more stationary while sitting on a bike than you are in other forms of aerobic exercise, it is easier to pay attention to your breathing and make sure that you are creating space in your rib cage for deep diaphragmatic breathing. It's important to connect your breath with the intensity of your workout. Always remember that you are exercising to increase your energy, not to deplete it.

Remember to calculate your working heart rate, and to check your heart rate every 10 minutes to make sure you work in your training zone (see Chapter 2).

Safety, Caution & Rest

Make sure that your bike is taken care of. Just like your body, your bike needs a good tune-up every now and then, so make sure you check it. If it's a bike at the gym, make sure that they maintain the bike so you don't get injured.

Make sure you get adequate rest and cross-train with other aerobic endurance activities. This way you engage and impact your muscles in different ways, moving further toward *your* best body ever!

Exercise Selection: Group Fitness Classes

If you wish to try a group class, you can choose from step aerobics and dance aerobics. Here are some guidelines if you choose a group exercise class or an exercise video for step aerobics and dance aerobics. Be sure to:

▲ Choose a class level that is right for you.

▲ Let your instructor know if you've never participated in a full body movement class before.

The following problems can occur with step aerobics, dance aerobics, and kickboxing:

▲ sore feet, ankles, knees, lower back, hip flexors

▲ shin splints, twisted ankle

Yoga Category

For this activity there is no particular yoga category you can identify with since the actions in step and dance aerobics involve moving from place to place. But the principles of vinyasa, connecting movement with movement—and breath with movement—are of great help. Since the body is erect most of the time, the standing balancing postures are helpful too.

Overtaxed muscles that need flexibility: Sore feet, ankles, knees, lower back, hip flexors, shins, ankles

Underutilized muscles that need strength: Upper body, thigh muscles to protect ankles, knees, feet

The warm-up

Step aerobics and dance aerobics classes incorporate a warm-up and a warm-down as part of the class, but very rarely is there any real emphasis on stretching in the warm-down. Even if there is, it is helpful to perform a couple of Sun Salutations before and/or after class.

The warm-down

Counter pose category: seated postures from the categories of forward bending, backward bending and twisting.

It's important to do both forward bending and backward bending postures to balance and strengthen the muscles of the front and back body. Side lateral bends and twists are important too for hip and spinal flexibility. Core strength.

The stronger your upper body is the more your legs can work. A combination of strength and flexibility in your legs is going to help your upper body to relax. And with a strong core in between will bridge both to work together in unison.

Group Aerobics Posture/Technique

There is nothing stationary about step or dance aerobics. In these classes things happen very quickly and choreography is involved. Leg and arm movements are interchanged. Awareness of your posture is crucial for avoiding injuries in this multi-directional movement activity. A balance of strength and flexibility is needed.

In step aerobics and dance aerobics you are constantly moving and adapting your posture according to what your body is doing, so you are constantly challenged to match your posture to the movements. The yoga poses most related to these types of classes are Standing Balancing postures together with the principles of flow, since you are connecting dance moves and moving in different directions.

The great thing is you are moving forward, backwards and sideways. In these classes, use both the legs and the arms. But I often see little involvement of the arms and a lack of full body integration.

Lower Body

You need to ground yourself from the feet to the pelvis and lengthen yourself from the pelvis to the crown of your head.

The impact on the feet is higher in a dance aerobics class than in a step class. It's important you are aware of the placement of your feet when stepping on the step. Make sure your whole foot steps onto the platform. Make sure to make use of the heel, to not be on the ball of the foot.

Upper Body

It's important to stretch your hip flexors consistently, since the hip flexors often get tight from all the leg lifting. Strong and flexible core muscles will help support your lower back and remind you to be mindful of the positioning of your pelvis and spine.

You will need to coordinate arm movement, and if you find that confusing, it can affect your breathing. Use the principle of yoga to pay attention to one thing at a time. Make sure you are breathing, and try to slow down as much as you can so you are still breathing as you learn. If there are both foot and arm movements, focus on the feet first and then try the arms. Relax the upper body and keep your hands on your hips, so you are sure you are breathing and keep the length in your spine.

Focus

Classes usually last for 1 hour including the warm-up and warm-down. The focus is usually in front of you (a mirror). Your neck should be long and you should feel yourself stretched through the crown of your head. Feel your focus stretches throughout your whole body.

Flow and Energy

It is a great feeling when you feel connected and are flowing with the movement, breath, and music. Your movement should be light and enjoyable. These types of classes are multi-directional. You move forward, backward, side laterally, up and down (on the step), do kicks, and even jumps. The intensity depends on the choreography and the level of the class.

Make sure you choose a class according to your level. If you don't have much coordination you might not want to choose a class that involves too much choreography. Rather choose one that is basic but works you mind, body, and soul.

Safety, Caution and Rest

Choose a class level that is for you. If you've never done a group class let your instructor know. Show up on time so you get the warm-up and try to stay the whole class so you get to warm-down as well.

CHAPTER 4

Welcome to Level 2

Level 2 is where you should start if:

▲ you have successfully completed Level 1

▲ you are currently working out and know all of the yoga postures and strength training exercises in Level 1

▲ you want to learn how to continue integrating the three elements of physical fitness into a balanced program for optimal fitness

In this second level of the Goa System you will build on your flexibility, strength, and endurance foundation from the first level.

▲ Yoga flexibility postures are added to further challenge your balance. In this level you will practice ribcage breathing (diaphragmatic breathing). This type of breathing together with the yoga postures will increase your flexibility and help deepen your breath. You will be introduced to a new yoga category; inverted postures and more arm balancing postures will be added.

▲ The strength training exercises with machine weights and dumbbells will challenge you to progressively increase resistance to improve your strength and stability. You will be introduced to the stability ball, which will challenge your stabilization muscles and increase core strength.

▲ The aerobic exercises will further increase your endurance by increasing your time and intensity. You can continue with power walking, biking, aerobic dance, or step aerobics from Level 1 and choose new activities like running and the elliptical trainer.

To do the Level 2 program, plan to do four 75-minute workouts per week. The charts below give you guildelines for which exercises to do for how long. Follow the 4-week program structure provided for this level. Within the general guidelines, adjust to a level of activity, intensity, and duration that works for you and your lifestyle.

Yoga Flexibility Program
New *From Level 1*

YOGA POSTURE CATEGORY	YOGA POSTURE	REPS EACH SIDE/BREATH CYCLES/TOTAL APPROX. TIME
Warm-Up/Warm-Down	*Sun Salutation A* Sun Salutation B	2 reps of each Sun Salutation/$^1/_2$ breath cycle for each yoga posture, except 3–5 breath cycles in Downward Facing Dog/5 minutes
Standing Balancing		
On both feet	Fierce pose	Part of Sun Salutation B
	Warrior 1	Part of Sun Salutation B
Side lateral bend	*Triangle pose*	1 rep/5 breath cycles/1 minute
Twist	Twisted Fierce pose	1 rep/5 breath cycles/1 minute
	Rotated Triangle pose	1 rep/5 breath cycles/1 minute
On one foot	Eagle pose	1 rep/5 breath cycles/1 minute
	Tree pose	1 rep/5 breath cycles/1 minute
Arm balancing	Side Plank pose	1 rep/5 breath cycles/1 minute
	Crow Pose	1 rep/5 breath cycles/30 seconds
Seated	Stick pose	1 rep/5 breath cycles/30 seconds
Forward bending	Back Stretching pose	1 rep/5 breath cycles/30 seconds
	Bound Angle pose	1 rep/5 breath cycles/30 seconds
	Cow's Face pose	1 rep/5 breath cycles/30 seconds

(Continued)

Yoga Flexibility Program (*Continued*)

YOGA POSTURE CATEGORY	YOGA POSTURE	REPS EACH SIDE/BREATH CYCLES/TOTAL APPROX. TIME
	Child's pose	1 rep/5 breath cycles/30 seconds
Twist	Marichyasana C	1 rep/5 breath cycles/1 minute
Backward bending	Bow pose	1 rep/5 breath cycles/1 minute
	Locust pose	1 rep/5 breath cycles/30 seconds
	Half Frog pose	1 rep/5 breath cycles/1 minute
Inverted	Shoulder stand	1 rep/10-20 breath cycles/1–3 minutes
Relaxation	Savasana	4 minutes

Strength-Training Program

New *From Level 1* (You can choose to integrate them into the Level 2 strength program depending on your time and energy)

EQUIPMENT	BODY PART	EXERCISE	SETS/REPS/APPROX. TIME
Dumb bells	Legs	Walking lunges	2 sets/15 reps/2 minutes
Stability ball		Stability bridge	2 sets/15 reps/3 minutes
Machine		Leg curl	2 sets/15 reps/2 minutes
		Leg extension	2 sets/15 reps/2 minutes
		Leg press	2 sets/15 reps/2 minutes
Stability ball	Core	Stability tail lift	2 sets/15 reps/2 minutes
		Stability plank/Bi-lateral pull-in	2 sets/15 reps/3 minutes
		Stability oblique bend	2 sets/15 reps/4 minutes
Body weight		Basic crunch	2 sets/15 reps/3 minutes

(*Continued*)

Strength-Training Program (*Continued*)

EQUIPMENT	BODY PART	EXERCISE	SETS/REPS/APPROX. TIME
		Basic oblique rotation	2 sets/15 reps/3 minutes
Machine	Back	*Seated row*	2 sets/15 reps/2 minutes
Tubing		*Standing row*	2 sets/15 reps/2 minutes
Dumb bells	Chest	*Chest fly*	2 sets/15 reps/2 minutes
Tubing		*Standing chest press*	2 sets/15 reps/2 minutes
Dumb bells	Shoulder	*Shoulder press*	2 sets/15 reps/2 minutes
		Side lateral raise	2 sets/15 reps/2 minutes
	Rotator cuff	*Horizontal shoulder internal rotation*	2 sets/15 reps/2 minutes
		Seated shoulder external rotation	2 sets/15 reps/2 minutes
	Biceps	*Bicep curl*	2 sets/15 reps/2 minutes
Tubing		*Standing biceps curl*	2 sets/15 reps/2 minutes
	Triceps	*Supine triceps extension*	2 sets/15 reps/2 minutes
Tubing		*Standing triceps extension*	2 sets/15 reps/2 minutes

Endurance Program

EXERCISE	TIME
Running	30 minutes
Elliptical trainer	30 minutes
Power walk/run	30 minutes
Biking	30 minutes

The 4 week program structure

Week	1	2	3	4
Structure	Cardio, legs, chest, back, core, yoga	Cardio, shoulders, biceps, triceps, core, yoga	Yoga day	Cardio: circuit training: Chest, back, shoulders, biceps, triceps, core, yoga
Cardio	Your choice	Your choice		Your choice
Yoga flex	Sun Salutation A	Sun Salutation A	Sun Salutation A	Sun Salutation A
	Sun Salutation B	Sun Salutation B	Sun Salutation B	Sun Salutation B
			Side plank	
			Triangle pose	
			Rotated Triangle pose	
			Tree pose	
Strength			Eagle pose	
	Leg press	Shoulder press	Crow pose	Walking lunges
	Leg extension	Side lateral raise		Stability bridge
	Leg curl	Horizontal shoulder internal rotation		Leg extension Leg curl
	Seated row	Seated shoulder external rotation		Seated row
	Chest fly	Biceps curl		Chest fly
		Supine triceps extension		

(Continued)

The 4 week program structure (*Continued*)

Week	1	2	3	4
Core	Basic crunch	Stability tail lift		Basic crunch
	Stability oblique bend	Stability plank		Stability oblique bend
		Bi-lateral pull-in		
Yoga	Stick pose	Stick pose	Stick pose	Stick pose
	Back stretching pose	Reclined extended hand to big toe pose	Reclined extended hand to big toe pose	Back stretching pose
	Bound Angle pose	Cow's Face pose	Cow's Face pose	Bound Angle pose
	Marichyasana C	Marichyasana C	Marichyasana C	Marichyasana C
			Half Frog pose	
	Locust pose	Locust pose	Locust pose	Locust pose
	Bow pose	Bow pose	Bow pose	Bow pose
	Child's pose	Child's pose	Child's pose Back stretching pose	Child's pose
	Savasana	Savasana	Shoulder stand	Savasana
			Fish pose	
			Savasana	

Level 2 Yoga

WARMING UP

SUN SALUTATION B

You got a nice taste of the Sun Salutation in Level 1. Now we're going to add to that with Sun Salutation B, which is a "step up." Sun Salutation B builds on integrated strength, and increases your endurance and calmness under pressure. It enlarges hip flexibility and creates lightness in the body, helping to detoxify both mental and physical impurities. This Sun Salutation will further ground, center, expand and lengthen you, all while building greater health.

Sun Salutation B teaches you to be specific; meaning, it is important to place your arms and legs in the right place. Once you do (even if it is hard in the beginning) the energy starts to flow and what was weak becomes stronger, what was inflexible becomes more flexible, what was out of balance becomes more in balance. You stand taller and feel more physically grounded because you are better aligned.

Did you try to use Sun Salutation A for your warm-up and warm-down in Level 1? I hope so.

It takes some time to wrap your mind around incorporating all aspects of this workout, but as you do, your workouts will become more balanced. You'll continue using the Sun Salutations for your warm-up in Level 2 only adding the postures of Sun Salutation B. You need to learn two new yoga positions: Fierce pose and Warrior 1. Again, it's important to experiment with the poses to customize them to your level and ability at this point. Remember, it's about what you can do now. Grow from where you are, not from where you think you should be. Get an idea of where you are heading and work yourself in that direction.

First, familiarize yourself with the individual poses, then "try them on" by breathing into them and finding the position that feels good. Next, when you feel comfortable with each individual pose, work on connecting them. Last, connect the breath with the movements. Enjoy—you have another opportunity to rise further with the sun!

Fierce Pose

Fierce Pose (also called Chair pose) is part of Sun Salutation B, but can also be used individually.

Benefit: Fierce pose is primarily a strength pose. It creates strength in the lower body muscles, belly, and spine. Fierce pose also stimulates the internal organs, diaphragm, and heart and helps expand and deepen your breath (you have no choice but to breathe deep in this pose). Whether you feel fierce or not, this pose will bring fierceness out of you—always with a chair handy for added support!

Fierce pose strengthens: Upper back muscles (trapezius, rhomboids), core (transverse abdominis), spine (upper, middle, lower), biceps, quadriceps, buttocks, ankles, shins

Fierce pose stretches: Calves, ankles, shoulders, chest, latissimus dorsi

Complementary strength exercises: Leg press, squat

Complementary yoga postures: Downward-Facing Dog pose, Upward-Facing Dog pose, Low Lunge pose

From Attention pose, inhale as you bend your knees and hips into a squat position (imagine yourself bending to sit in a chair) with your arms straight down at your sides. Separate your arms to turn your palms facing the sky and extend them up alongside your ears. You can either keep the palms together or separate them to shoulder-width apart. Inhale as you return to Attention pose. On the return, imagine someone pulling you through the crown of your head to lift as a unit. As part of the Sun Salutation B, you will inhale into the Fierce pose, then exhale into a standing forward bend (from Sun Salutation A).

Modification

Exhale   Inhale   Inhale   Inhale   Exhale

Breath/Focus: This is a powerful pose so the more your expand your breath and the deeper you breathe the easier it is and the more you'll get out of it. Stretch your focus beyond your thumbs while reminding yourself of how fierce you are.

Ground: You are grounding from the feet. Lift and spread your toes, then release them to the floor. This helps you lean into your heels and puts the pressure on your thigh muscles rather than your knee joints.

Center: Allow the pelvis to rotate back slightly without arching your lower spine. Keep your belly actively involved.

Expand: Lift your breastbone and notice an expansive feeling through your chest and rib cage. Keep your shoulders away from your ears. Draw the shoulder blades down. Your neck should be able to move freely.

Lengthen: The lower body should feel a little heavy and the upper body slightly light. Once the legs are grounded you should feel lengthened from your tailbone to the crown of your head. Reach evenly through both arms and adjust them as needed. Feel the extension all the way through your fingertips.

Warrior I

Benefit: Warrior 1 is primarily a strength pose. It creates strength in the lower body muscles, core, spine, shoulders, and arms. Warrior 1 also stimulates the internal organs, diaphragm, and heart and expands and deepens your breath. It brings clarity of the mind and calms the brain. Warriors are in control of themselves. This pose will give you the self-control to do whatever you desire.

Warrior 1 strengthens: Quadriceps, hamstrings, buttocks, calf, shoulders (front/middle), upper back (trapezius), core (transverse abdominis), spine (lower, middle, upper)

Warrior 1 stretches: Hip flexors, chest, upper back (latissimus dorsi)

Complementary strength training: Leg press, leg extension, leg curl

Complementary yoga postures: Fierce pose, Arm Raise pose

From Downward-Facing Dog pose, inhale as you step your right leg forward into Low Lunge, then exhale as you pivot your left heel in so that your foot is placed at a 45-degree angle. Make sure that the outer edge of your foot is grounded. Inhale as you lift your torso to a vertical line and extend your arms toward the ceiling, either shoulder-width apart or with palms together. Make sure your right knee is bent and parallel with your ankle and that your left leg is extended with the foot grounded. Gaze toward your thumbs. Hold this position for several breath cycles to feel the pose. Exhale as you lower your arms to the floor into Low Lunge pose, inhale to Plank pose, exhale to Chaturanga (or Cobra pose), inhale to Upward-Facing Dog pose, and, last, exhale back to Downward-Facing Dog pose.

Repeat Warrior 1 using your left side by starting with stepping the left leg forward into Low Lunge. When you have completed the left side, holding it for several breaths in Warrior 1, continue to repeat the same flow back to Downward-Facing Dog pose. Study the Sun Salutation B flow chart on the following page, and start practicing it. Do it slowly at first, taking it step by step—you can do it.

FOCUS ON FORM

Breath/Focus: Even if you find it challenging to match the breathing with the poses, make sure you are not holding your breath. You are stretching your lungs and expanding your life force. Being the warrior you are, you will integrate with patience and determination.

Ground: You are grounding through the feet. All 10 toes are spread; front foot is parallel and back foot is turned in. Front heel should be in the arch of the back foot. Make sure you evenly distribute your weight over both the right and left legs.

| Exhale | Inhale/Exhale | Inhale | Exhale | Inhale | Exhale | Inhale | Exhale | Repeat on left leg |

Center: As you lift your spine to vertical, draw your tailbone under a little bit to make sure you feel length in your lower back and spine, and keep your belly active.

Expand: Lift your breastbone and feel your torso open and expand. Relax your shoulders and draw your shoulder blades down as you reach evenly through both arms and feel the extension to your fingertips. It's important to keep your spine vertical and not leaning over the front bent leg. Feel free to adjust your arms (up or down) according to how your shoulders, neck, and breath feel.

Lengthen: Lengthen from the tailbone to the crown of your head and from the shoulders to the fingertips.

COMPLETING SUN SALUTATION B

Now you can practice the flow of Sun Salutation B:

| Exhale | Inhale | Exhale | Inhale | Exhale | Inhale | Exhale | Inhale | Exhale |

Right leg

| Inhale | Exhale | Inhale | Exhale | Inhale | Exhale |

left leg

| Inhale | Exhale | Inhale | Exhale | Inhale | Exhale/Inhale 3–5 breath cycles |

| Inhale/Exhale | Inhale | Exhale | Inhale | Exhale |

BALANCING ON BOTH FEET

What do you think of standing and balancing on both your feet? These poses are pretty challenging at first, but you will quickly progress with regular practice. Just remind yourself of how strong and balanced they make you feel. If your muscles are tight, these postures will add flexibility. If you are already flexible, standing postures will give you strength and stability. A strong base will make you feel in better control and help you get maximum results with minimum strain and effort.

A strong base will also help you extend yourself through your torso, making it easier for the breath to pass through effortlessly. By making your body as open as possible, you'll relax more, creating balance and enabling you to work deeper into the standing postures. Overall awareness of your lower body will lead to greater awareness of your upper body.

By standing taller you are able to engage your core muscles and breathe fully to balance better. This way you avoid grasping with the toes, which often happens when you lose your balance. Be very generous with the breath during the standing postures; it will not help you to balance better if you hold your breath.

STANDING TWISTING

Twisted Fierce Pose

Benefit: Twisted Fierce pose gives you both strength and flexibility. It's a very powerful pose that increases vitality, cleanses, purifies the internal organs and keeps the core muscles strong but flexible. How refreshing it can be to twist!

Twisted Fierce pose strengthens: Quadriceps, buttocks, ankles, shins, core (transverse abdominals), chest, biceps

Twisted Fierce pose stretches: Upper back (latissimus dorsi), core (obliques), shoulders (rear), triceps

Complementary strength exercises: Leg press, squat

Complementary yoga postures: Fierce pose, Rotated Triangle pose

Inhale into fierce pose and exhale as you rotate your left elbow to the outside of your right thigh with palms together in prayer position. Make sure your knees are parallel and keep them together. Turn your head right and gaze toward the sky. Stay in the pose for about 5 breath cycles. Keep working the twist so that you can eventually (if you're not already there) extend your left arm to the outside of your right thigh to place the left palm of your hand on the floor and reach your right arm to the sky.

Inhale as you rewind back into Fierce pose, then exhale to Attention pose.

FOCUS ON FORM

Breath/Focus: Don't struggle or force the twisting; just keep the breath flowing through you. Pay attention to how your body responds to the pose and adjust yourself according to how you feel and how your breath sounds.

Ground: You are grounding from your feet. Make sure you are leaning into your heels, keeping your toes spread. Keep your knees together. If one knee is behind the other, you are rotating more from your hips than your midback.

Center: By keeping the knees in place and engaging your belly you will better be able to center through your pelvis and create stability in your lower spine and back.

| Exhale | Inhale | Exhale | Exhale | Inhale | Inhale | Exhale |

Expand: Keep your rib cage lifted by feeling the twist from the bottom of your ribs (midback). Your breastbone is lifted, your shoulders are relaxed, and your shoulder blades are drawn toward each other.

Lengthen: You are lengthening from the tailbone to the crown of your head. Maintain the extension even as you rotate.

BALANCING ON ONE FOOT

It is a little more challenging to balance on one foot, but you can do it. Keep building on what you have already practiced in Level 1. Take your time, breathe, extend yourself, and try to stay relaxed. Balance takes practice and happens over time. That's how you build a strong foundation (even on one leg!).

Eagle Pose

Benefit: Eagle pose creates strength, flexibility, and endurance. It deepens concentration and calms the mind, so that you can find stillness in the midst of your daily commotion.

You might feel more like a New York pretzel than an eagle, but that's not a bad thing.

Eagle pose strengthens: Core (transverse abdominis); bent leg: quadriceps, buttocks, hamstring, shins, ankle, foot

Eagle pose stretches: Spine, upper back (trapezius, rhomboids), shoulders (rear), triceps; crossed leg: outer thigh, hip, ankle, foot

Complementary strength exercises: Leg press, squat, tail lift

Complementary yoga posture: Fierce pose

Exhale   Inhale   Exhale   Inhale/Exhale   Exhale

From Attention pose, lean into a semisquat position (as you did in Fierce pose), keeping your arms shoulder-height, extended to the side. Lift your right knee toward your chest and cross the right leg over your left leg. Wrap the right leg around your left lower leg and see if you can hook your right big toe on the inside of your left ankle. If you can't, keep working at it until you can. Bend your elbows and cross your left arm on top of your right arm and then wrap your arms into a prayer position. Once you are stable in this position, try to hinge at the hips and lean forward over your thighs. Keep your focus forward (if lifted) and toward the floor (if bending) and breathe 5 deep breath cycles. Inhale as you rewind out of the pose and exhale back into Attention pose. Repeat using your left side.

FOCUS ON FORM

Breath/Focus: Relax your face and your eyes as you remind yourself that in order to take off and fly high you first must ground yourself. If you fall (it happens to all of us), take it lightly!

Ground: You are grounding from your feet. Spread your right toes and balance evenly on the foot. Lean into the heel as you did in Fierce pose to take your weight off the knee.

Center: Don't twist the pelvis! Adjust your pelvis and engage your belly to get the support you need.

Expand: Lift your breastbone and roll your shoulders back as you work your elbows to shoulder height. Try to move your hands away from your face.

Lengthen: You are lengthened from your tailbone to the crown of your head.

ARM BALANCING

Having fun yet? It is important you have fun with the arm balancing poses as you get more comfortable transferring your balance and grounding yourself on your hands versus your feet. Just practice them consistently. Where there is a will there is a way! As mentioned in Level 1, if you have wrist problems, however, the arm balancing poses might be difficult for you. A great tool I've found is called the Gripitz. This helps protect your wrists as they become stronger (check the resource guide at the back of the book).

Side Plank Pose

Benefit: Side plank pose is the "sister pose" of Plank pose, and is mostly a strength pose. It integrates the body into a whole and balances the interaction between the front body and back body muscles. Because of its lateral nature, it also strengthens each side of your body independently.

Side Plank pose strengthens: Upper back (trapezius, rhomboids), shoulders (side), triceps, wrists, hands, core (transverse abdominis, obliques), outer thigh, inner thigh, shins, ankles, spine

Side plank pose stretches: Chest, biceps, shoulder (anterior)

Complementary strength exercises: Side lateral raise, supine triceps extension, outer thigh, inner thigh, stability oblique bend

Complementary yoga posture: Triangle pose, plank pose

From Plank pose turn to your right side (right arm). Keep both feet flexed and try to place your left foot on top of your right foot. Lift your breastbone and roll your shoulders open as you extend your left arm toward the sky. Turn your head and gaze at your left fingertips. If you find yourself sinking into your right hip, try to lift the hip up and engage your right oblique more, or try lowering your right shin to the floor for support. If you are stable enough to take it farther, lift your left leg and hold it no higher than your hip or take hold of your big toe and extend the leg toward the sky.

Modification

Inhale   Exhale   Inhale/Exhale Exhale/Inhale Exhale/Inhale   Exhale   Inhale/Exhale

Stay in the position you can support for about 5 breath cycles. Return to Plank pose and repeat using the left side. When complete, inhale and return to Plank pose, exhale to Downward-Facing Dog pose, and finish off as if it were Sun Salutation A.

FOCUS ON FORM

Breath/Focus: Breathe full breaths in the position. If you cannot breathe fully, you need to adjust your position so that you can. Draw your awareness throughout your whole body, particularly to your pelvis and rib cage. Think Attention pose sideways!

Ground: You are grounding through the side of your foot and palm of your hand. Keep your fingers spread and your feet flexed and press the palm of your hand into the floor.

Center: Your pelvis is in a neutral position. It's important to engage your core (especially the transverse and oblique) in this position to avoid sinking into your hip.

Expand: Keep your breastbone lifted, relax your shoulders, and draw your shoulder blades together. Allow your back muscles to support you. Expand your rib cage so your lungs can expand and your heart can lift.

Lengthen: First lengthen from your tailbone through your spine to the crown of your head. Then feel the extension from your feet to the crown of your head.

Crow Pose

Benefits: Crow pose is mostly a strength pose for the arms, wrists, and core, but it also opens the groin and tones the internal organs. Crow pose balances the nervous system and improves your sense of physical balance.

Crow pose strengthens: Arms (biceps,

triceps, wrists, forearms), core (transverse abdominis), serratus anterior, shoulders, upper back muscles, chest

Crow pose stretches: Spine, groin

Complementary strength exercises: Tail lift, supine triceps extension, biceps curl, chest press, seated row

Complementary yoga postures: Warrior 1 and 2, Fierce pose and Fierce pose twist, Bound Angle pose, Plank pose

From Standing Forward Bending pose with arms shoulder-width apart and the palms of your hands on the floor, place your knees on your upper arms and lift your hips. Your objective here is to find a "shelf" for your knees to rest on so you can lift your feet off the floor into the Crow pose. Over time and with practice, you can lean forward with the weight of your body supported by your arms and lift one foot off the floor at a time until your upper body and arms can support you doing the full crow pose. Do not throw your legs up; move with control and patience. After lots of practice you'll be able to do this automatically.

When you're stable in the Crow pose, hold it for about 5 breath cycles. Then step one foot back at a time (or jump back when you're better skilled) into Plank pose and finish off as if it's a Sun Salutation A.

FOCUS ON FORM

Breath/Focus: Breathing is deep and steady. Keep focusing on the floor in front of you.

Ground: You are grounding from your arms and hands.

Center: Keep your core muscles active to center through your pelvis. This will help you create the connection and lightness you need to balance and "take off."

Exhale   Inhale/Exhale   Inhale   Exhale

Expand: Lift your breastbone to create expansion in your rib cage. Relax your shoulders and draw your shoulder blades together while breathing.

Lengthen: The spine is naturally more rounded in this position, but within this rounding it should be elongated, not hunched.

SEATED POSTURES

As mentioned in Level 1 the standing postures are demanding, but the seated postures are more challenging. I find them more challenging because they are not as much fun as the standing postures. The seated postures can seem static, boring, and "cool" (because they are more stationary) compared to the moving, energetic, "hot" standing postures.

If you are stiff, these poses will challenge your ego and patience. You just can't fake the flexibility in seated postures. Remind yourself that this is about *becoming* flexible—and you are! In the standing postures you can get away without having a lot of flexibility.

If you are very flexible these are going to seem very easy. Nevertheless, they are certainly necessary and if you don't like them now, you'll learn to love them, as I have.

Stick Pose

Benefit: Stick pose is a whole body isometric posture which requires both strength and flexibility. It connects the upper and lower extremities and builds all-around strength in the torso. Upper back strength must be matched with core abdominal strength. This is a very basic pose, but try to hold it for 3 minutes and you'll notice which muscles are strong and which are weak.

Stick pose strengthens: Upper back muscles (trapezius, rhomboids, latissimus dorsi), core (transverse abdominis, erector spinae), triceps, quadriceps, shins

Stick pose stretches: Chest, shoulders (anterior), spine, rib cage

Complementary strength exercises: Seated row, stability tail lift

Complementary yoga postures: Sun Salutation B, Locust pose

Sit on the floor holding your spine in a vertical position with your legs extended in front of you and feet flexed. Focus on a spot in front of you. Keep your arms next to your hips and press the palms of your hands against the floor to create lift in the rib cage. This will make room for breathing.

If your hamstrings, hip flexors, and lower back are tight, bend your legs and sit on a folded blanket or towel. Work on extending the spine first and foremost; the hamstrings will follow. Hold for about 5 to 10 breath cycles before moving into the next posture.

FOCUS ON FORM

Breath/Focus: Breathe deeply as you pay attention to how your posture is affected by this pose and adjust yourself accordingly.

Ground: You are grounding through your pelvis. Move your buttocks so that you sit on your sitting bones.

Center: Allow the tailbone to move backwards a little to maintain a slight anterior tilt in the pelvis.

Expand: Lift your breastbone, keep your shoulders relaxed, draw your shoulder blades together, and draw your chin slightly in. In order to get extension in your spine, ground the pelvis so that you can lift your rib cage out of your hips—not an easy thing to do if your hip flexors, hamstrings, and lower back are tight. Try to visualize your buttocks glued to the floor. Imagine that a person came from behind, wrapped his or her arms around your rib cage and tried to lift you off the floor.

Modification

Inhale/Exhale Inhale/Exhale

It should feel as if your rib cage is lifting out of your hips. That's the feeling you are after.

Lengthen: You are lengthening from your tailbone to the crown of your head. Feel the length through your spine.

Seated Forward Bending Postures

Back-Stretching Pose

Benefit: Back-stretching pose (also called Seated Forward Bending pose) is mostly a flexibility pose. It stretches the hip joints and the muscles in the back body, particularly the hamstrings. Releasing the tension in the back body helps a distracted mind release mental tension and become more present.

Be cautious if you have a serious back or spine injury. Perform this pose only under the supervision of an experienced teacher and consult your physician. Do the modified version by bending your legs and avoid bending forward completely, or use the Reclined Extended Hand to Big Toe pose from Level 1.

Back-stretching pose strengthens: Quadriceps, shins, core (transverse abdominis), biceps

Back-stretching pose stretches: Hamstrings, calves, entire spine

Complementary strength exercises: Hamstring curl

Complementary yoga postures: Standing Forward Bending pose, Downward-Facing Dog pose

Modification

Inhale   Exhale   Exhale   Inhale/Exhale

From Stick pose, inhale deeply as you prepare yourself to hinge forward from your hips. Exhale as you bend forward to take hold of your feet. If your hamstrings and lower back are tight, bend your legs to maintain the length of your spine. If your hamstrings are long, keep your legs extended with your quadriceps contracted. Hold the pose for 5 to 10 breath cycles. Stay with the breath and try to relax the tension in your hamstrings. Inhale as you lift out of the pose. Exhale and return to Stick pose. Inhale as you lift up; exhale as you return to Stick pose.

FOCUS ON FORM

Breath/Focus: Your exhales help lengthen your hamstrings and spine, allowing you to move deeper into the bend. Keep your gaze toward your big toes while paying attention to your upper body. Avoid moving into hunchback mode.

Ground: Your are grounding through your pelvis.

Center: Allow the tailbone to move backwards a little to maintain a slight anterior tilt in the pelvis. This prevents you from overstretching your lower back muscles.

Expand: As you bend forward, keep your breastbone lifted and your shoulders relaxed and rolled back, and draw your shoulder blades into your back.

Lengthen: You are first and foremost lengthening from your tailbone to the crown of your head. Avoid dropping your head to the thighs. As you create length in your spine, your hamstrings will follow.

Bound Angle Pose

Benefit: Bound Angle pose is primarily a flexibility pose, with some strength involved in the core and upper back muscles. It opens the groin and hips, and helps remove some of the tiredness you feel from a lot of standing and walking.

Bound Angle pose strengthens (when spine is vertical): Core muscles (transverse abdominis, erector spinae), upper back muscles (trapezius, rhomboids), biceps

Bound Angle pose stretches (when bending forward): Entire spine, inner thighs, ankles, feet

Complementary strength exercises: Inner thigh

Complementary yoga postures: Warrior 1, Reclined Hand to Big Toe pose (open to side), Triangle pose

From Stick pose bend your legs to bring the soles of your feet together and draw your feet as close to your groin as possible. Open the soles of your feet like a book. Inhale as you straighten up and exhale as you hinge forward from your hips as far as your inner thighs allow you to go. Hold the pose for 5 to 10 breath cycles. Inhale as you return to a vertical position and exhale to Stick pose.

FOCUS ON FORM

Breath/Focus: Keep your focus at a spot in front of you, breathe deeply, and move farther forward as your inner thighs open.

Ground: You are grounding from your pelvis. It's not easy to get grounded in this position unless you get lift in your spine.

Center: Your core muscles must be active to ground and support you. Allow the tailbone to move backwards a little to maintain a slight anterior tilt in the pelvis. This prevents you from overstretching your lower back muscles.

Expand: While holding onto the insides of your feet, keep your arms extended and close to your waist; they will support you in lifting your breastbone. Keep your shoulders relaxed and draw your shoulder blades into your back. As you bend forward, pull your elbows backwards by engaging your biceps.

Inhale/Exhale   Inhale   Exhale   Inhale   Exhale

Lengthen: You are lengthening from your tailbone to the crown of your head while working the natural curves of your spine. Hunching or dropping your head to the floor will not help stretch your inner thighs! That will only stretch your upper back. Lift tall as you bend forward, and fully exhale.

Cow's Face Pose

Benefit: Cow's Face pose is primarily a flexibility posture with some strength involved in the upper back. It alleviates anxiety, tension, and fatigue and is great for relaxing the mind. Cow's Face pose makes the legs and hips more supple and releases stiffness in the upper body; it's also great for improving your physical posture.

Cows' Face Pose strengthens (when spine is vertical): Core muscles (transverse abdominis, erector spinae), upper back (trapezius, rhomboids)

Cows' Face Pose stretches: Triceps, shoulders, chest, buttocks, outer thigh, hips, ankles, and feet

Complementary strength exercises: Outer thigh, supine triceps extension

Complementary yoga postures: Downward-Facing Dog pose, Eagle pose, Fierce pose

From the stick pose, bend your knees and cross your right leg over the left by stacking the right knee on top of the left knee. Bring the right foot to the outside of the left hip and the left foot to the outside of the right hip. Sit evenly on your sitting bones. Inhale as you stretch your left arm to the ceiling and bend at the elbow to place your palm on your upper back (between your shoulder blades). Exhale as you use

Modification

Exhale   Inhale   Exhale/Inhale Exhale/Inhale Inhale/Exhale

your right hand to press your left elbow back so the palm slides further down between your shoulder blades. Inhale and extend your right arm to the floor as you rotate your palm to face backward (it will inwardly rotate your right shoulder), then exhale as you bend your right elbow to slide your right hand and fingers up along the spine to join the left fingers.

If your fingers don't join, use a towel or a rope to support you as you work yourself in that direction.

Breathe for 5 to 8 breath cycles on this side. Inhale as you release your hands or the towel/rope, and then exhale the hands on your hips. Repeat on the other side. You might be able to bind on one side and not the other side; that shows an imbalance in your shoulder flexibility.

FOCUS ON FORM

Breath/Focus: Keep your breath steady and even. Gaze at a spot in front of you while being aware of how your body responds.

Ground: You are grounding from your pelvis. Adjust your legs to make sure both sitting bones are grounded.

Center: Your are both grounding and centering through your pelvis. Keep your core muscles active to provide support and stabilization.

Expand: Core stabilization will help you lift your breastbone. Relax your shoulders so that you can keep your rib cage lifted out of your hips.

Lengthen: First and foremost, maintain length in your spine and breathe fully. The tightness in your arms and legs will release over time and with practice. Be sure to make yourself comfortable.

SEATED TWISTING POSTURES

Marichyasana C

Benefit: Marichyasana C is primarily a flexibility pose. It stretches and strengthens the spine, relieves mild back and hip pain, massages the internal organs, stretches the shoulders, and stimulates the brain.

Be cautious if you have a serious back or spine injury. Perform this pose only under the supervision of an experienced teacher and consult your physician. Modify as necessary.

Marichyasana C pose strengthens: Core muscles (transverse abdominis), upper back spine and back muscles (trapezius, latissimus dorsi), quadriceps (the extended leg)

Marichyasana C pose stretches: Outer thigh, core muscles (obliques, erector spinae), chest, shoulders

Complementary strength exercises: Stability oblique bend

Complementary yoga postures: Revolved Triangle pose, Reclined Spinal Twist pose

From Stick pose draw your right knee toward your chest with your right foot grounded to the floor. Your heel should be in front of your right sitting bone. Lift tall as you draw your right leg across your body and rotate your torso to the right. Your left arm either wraps around your right leg or extends to the outside. Gaze over your right shoulder at a spot behind you. If your left armpit is close to your right knee, try to bind by internally rotating your left shoulder to bend at the elbow and wrap your arm around the left knee to bind with the right arm. Find the position that works for you and hold for 5 to 10 breath cycles. Feel yourself growing taller on the inhalations and twist further on the exhalations. Inhale as you look forward and exhale as you release out of the pose. Repeat on the left side.

Modification Modification

Exhale   Inhale/Exhale   Inhale/Exhale   Inhale/Exhale   Exhale

FOCUS ON FORM

Breath/Focus: Twisting postures don't make it easy to breathe. That is why it is doubly important that you create length in your spine so you can make room for the breath.

Ground: You are grounding from your pelvis. In this position the right sitting bone might lift; just make sure you are twisting from your mid-back and not your lower back. The left extended leg is your anchor. Keep the foot flexed and the quadriceps contracted.

Center: Your are both grounding and centering through your pelvis. Keep the core muscles active for support and stabilization.

Expand: Lift your breastbone, relax your shoulders, and draw your shoulder blades toward each other, allowing you to twist from your midback.

Lengthen: If you find it challenging to create length in your upper spine, sit on a blanket or yoga block to improve circulation in your hips and lower back. Keep at it and you will find a way to make it work.

BACK-BENDING POSTURES

Bow Pose

Benefit: Bow pose is both a flexibility and a strength pose. It realigns the spinal column, improves your physical posture, massages the abdominal organs, relieves constipation, and improves blood circulation to the lower back and throughout the body.

Be cautious if you have any back or spine injury. Perform this pose only under the supervision of an experienced teacher, and consult your physician. Using Locust pose as a substitute for Bow pose will help you target the same area Bow pose does, but at a lower intensity.

Bow pose strengthens: Hamstrings, buttocks, core (erector spinae, transverse abdominis), upper back muscles (trapezius, rhomboids, latissimus dorsi), shoulders (rear)

Bow pose stretches: Front neck and shoulders, chest, core (rectus abdominis), hip flexors, quadriceps, shins, ankle

Complementary strength exercises: Hamstring curl, seated row

Complementary yoga postures: Locust pose, Upward-Facing Dog pose

Lie on your belly with your feet and legs together, arms beside your body. Bend your knees and take hold of the outside of your ankles with your hands while resting your forehead on the floor. Inhale as you lift your head, chest, and legs off the floor while pushing the feet away from the body, contracting your buttocks, hamstrings, and upper back muscles. Exhale at the top and stay there for about 5 breath cycles. Exhale as you lower to the floor. You can repeat this two to three times. Then counter pose with Child's pose for 5 breath cycles.

FOCUS ON FORM

Breath/Focus: At first it's challenging to breathe on your stomach—this is why it's very important to center and expand to help you lengthen and then lift yourself to create more space for breathing throughout your rib cage. Inhale as you lift; exhale as you lower. Keep your gaze in front of you.

Ground: You are grounding through your pelvis. Make sure you place your pelvis into a neutral position by drawing your pelvis under and pressing your pelvic bones into the floor.

Center: If your pelvis is positioned correctly there is no need to over-squeeze the buttocks. Keep the core muscles engaged for support and to avoid a "crunching" feeling in the lower back.

Exhale   Inhale   Exhale

Expand: Relax your shoulders, draw your shoulder blades together, and keep your breastbone lifted. Feel the lift and expansion from the bottom of your front ribs.

Lengthen: You are lengthening from your tailbone to the crown of your head. It's very important to get the extension of your body first. The moment you have your pelvis in the correct position, you'll be able to create length. The inhalation will naturally give you more lift. Avoid "crunching" the neck by throwing your head back.

Fish Pose

Benefit: Fish pose is primarily a flexibility pose. It opens the rib cage and encourages inhalations. Fish pose is used as a counter pose for a shoulder stand.
Be cautious if you have a back or spine injury. Perform this pose only under the supervision of an experienced teacher, and consult your physician. Do the modification shown using a yoga block for back support.

Fish pose strengthens: Upper back muscles (rhomboids, trapezius), biceps, core (transverse abdominis, erector spinae), quadriceps

Fish pose stretches: Chest, shoulders (anterior), neck (anterior), core (rectus abdominis), hip flexors

Complementary strength exercises: Seated row, biceps curl

Complementary yoga postures: Upward-Facing Dog pose, Bow pose

Modification Modification

Exhale   Inhale   Inhale   Inhale   Inhale/Exhale

Lie on your back with your arms alongside body. Inhale as you draw your shoulder blades together while you press your elbows and forearms into the floor to lift your spine off the floor. The top of your head is resting on the floor. Exhale at the top of the pose. If you find this hard on your spine you might want to place a yoga block under your shoulder blades and a folded blanket or towel under your head. A different option is to use a stability ball to help you open your spine, chest, and shoulders farther. Hold the pose for 5 to 10 breath cycles. Inhale and press your elbows and forearms against the floor to lift your head up. Draw your chin toward your chest and exhale as you roll onto the floor vertebra by vertebra.

FOCUS ON FORM

Breath/Focus: You must adjust yourself in this pose and puff up your chest to create space enough to breathe; this is not easy. You might feel a little uncomfortable until you are able to create the length you need.

Ground: You are grounding through your pelvis (your sitting bones) and forearms.

Center: You want to feel extension in your lower spine.

Expand: Relax your shoulders by keeping your shoulders away from your ears; draw your shoulder blades together and lift your breastbone.

Lengthen: Your flexibility will determine how much you'll be able to bend your arms to create length in your spine.

INVERTED POSTURES

Downward-Facing Dog pose has given you a taste of and prepared you for inverted postures. The inversions (often called "the fountain of youth") are basically standing postures in the reverse; they literally turn us upside down. By turning the body upside down we reverse blood flow and a rich supply of blood will flow into the brain to nourish neurons and flush out toxins.

Blood and lymph easily accumulate in the limbs and abdomen and are drained back to the head and circulated to the lungs, purified, and recirculated to all parts of the body. This whole process nourishes the cells of the entire system. Inversions calm the brain and relieve stress and mild depression. The pituitary gland balances and tunes the entire endocrine system. This increases concentration and reduces fatigue.

Inversions encourage correct breathing. The breath becomes slow and deep. You just can't hold your breath upside down. The internal organs get a super massage.

The inversion covered here is the shoulder stand. It might look a little intimidating at first, but when done correctly at your level there is very little pressure on either your head or shoulders. The inversion will give you a newfound respect for balance, alignment, and lightness—the shoulder stand demands nothing less than full body integration.

Practice with care: When you do the shoulderstand you *never* want to throw your legs up in the air. Don't take any chances. Take your time and engage from your core muscles You must work on building a foundation for these poses, and you must do it with patience.

Perform this pose under the supervision of an experienced teacher if you don't feel comfortable doing it on your own.

You should not practice inversions during menstruation (because of the reverse blood flow), if you have neck injuries, or if you are pregnant. Inverted postures are very beneficial but should be practiced with care. Never force yourself into the positions. Work at them over time and use the wall as your modification to ease your way into them.

Supported Shoulder Stand

Benefit: Shoulder stand is both a strength and a flexibility pose. It relieves stress since it calms your brain. Shoulder stand improves digestion and stimulates the thyroid, prostate gland, and internal organs. It also reduces fatigue, symptoms of menopause, and insomnia.

Shoulder stand strengthens: Upper back muscles (trapezius, rhomboids, latissimus dorsi), leg muscles, buttocks, core muscles, biceps, forearms, wrists

Shoulder stand stretches: Shoulders (anterior), chest, entire spine

Complementary strength exercise: Seated row

Complementary yoga postures: Bow pose, Back Stretching pose

This version of the Shoulder stand is performed with blanket support under the shoulders.

Move to the wall and place 1 to 3 folded blankets in a yoga mat about an arm's length from the wall. Lie down on your back with your head off the mat and shoulders at the edge of the folded blankets. Bend your knees and place your feet on the wall hip-width apart. Walk your feet up the wall as you lift your pelvis to place your hands on your back. Work your hands down toward your shoulders and work your elbows to shoulder-width apart, knees hip-width apart, and shinbones level.

As you feel comfortable in this position straighten one leg at a time. This places more weight on your shoulders without putting the pressure on your neck. You might not be able to position yourself into a complete vertical line. Work at a level that feels comfortable for you.

Stay in this position for 10 to 20 breath cycles. Counterpose with Fish pose for 5 breath cycles.

FOCUS ON FORM

Breath/Focus: Your breath should become deep and smooth in this posture. If the breath is shallow, you've moved too far into it—easy does it. Gaze toward your heart center and be mindful of how your body responds to being inverted. Adjust accordingly.

Modification

Exhale   Inhale   Inhale/Exhale   Inhale/Exhale   Exhale   Inhale/Exhale

Ground: You are grounding through your upper arms and shoulders. Avoid putting too much pressure on your neck. Place your hands on your lower back and keep your elbows shoulder-width apart. Keep your fingers spread and pointing upward; this puts less pressure on your wrists.

Center: Keep your core muscles engaged to avoid sinking into your pelvis and putting unnecessary pressure on your wrists. Your pelvis should be in a neutral position.

Expand: It is not easy to be inverted, but try to keep your breastbone lifted so that you can draw your shoulder blades toward each other.

Lengthen: You are lengthening through your spine, ultimately creating a vertical line from your shoulders to your toes.

RELAXATION

Are you getting more used to relaxing? Or has it been a challenge for you to take time out after your workouts to relax? Don't give up; some days may be better than others, but keep practicing consistently. Relaxation will give you renewed strength by making you more present.

The final relaxation posture, Savasana, is said to be the most challenging yoga pose. Obviously, this is not on a physical level, but more on a mental level. Anybody can lie down on the floor and look relaxed, but the mind is running 190 miles per hour (that can be very stressful). You don't want to *look* relaxed, you want to *feel* relaxed.

After you've positioned yourself into your Savasana position become a witness to your breath. Follow the inhalations and the exhalations. Try to notice where your breath goes, and where it stops. Be mindful of any distractions; for example, you might start thinking about what you are going to eat after your work-out, or something you forgot to do, an e-mail you have to send and so on.

Ask yourself if you really need to occupy your mind with the thought at this time? Can it wait? Or maybe you have to think it through and then "send" them away, saying to them you'll return later on.

Ask yourself whether the thoughts that occupy you give you energy or drain you of energy.

This is not a practice to make your mind blank, but more a practice of becoming/being aware of what distracts you. This is a time to clean out your mind and make space for renewed energy. How can you do that when your mind is clogged up with a million thoughts. So, over the course of this month just pay attention to first finding out where your mind is and then "clearing" it to create more room for new energy and growth.

Savasana

Lie on the floor on your back and close your eyes and mouth. Open your legs to about shoulder width, and let your feet naturally flip to the side. Keep your arms at your sides with your palms facing up. Lift your buttocks so you can adjust your lower back, and adjust your shoulders so both of your shoulder blades relax evenly on the floor. Keep your chin drawn toward your chest, so the back of your neck is long. If you find your neck arches too much, fold a towel and place it behind your head for support to ease tight neck muscles.

If your lower back feels uncomfortable, roll a blanket or towel and put it behind your knees to give extra support to your back. Put on extra clothes, or a comfy blanket to ensure you continue to stay warm. It's hard to relax when you are cold.

Strength Training

LOWER BODY

The lower body exercises in the Level 2 strength-training program will increase the strength and stability in your foundation—your leg muscles. The exercises will also target problem figure areas and help tone and define your thighs.

These leg exercises are a great complement to Sun Salutation B and the standing balancing postures. They also help prevent injuries in your endurance training.

DUMBBELLS

Walking Lunges

Benefit: The walking lunges exercise is a great shaper and toner for the lower body muscles. It is fun to do and beneficial for balance, coordination, strength, and endurance as well. Just as in the squat, proper alignment is essential for results.

Muscles being strengthened: Quadriceps, buttocks, hamstrings, shins, ankles, core (transverse abdominis, erector spinae)

Complementary strength poses: Standing postures and in particular, Warrior 1

Complementary flexibility poses: Reclined Extended Hand to Big Toe pose, Half Frog pose

From ready position, hold the dumbbells in your hands with your arms at your sides while focusing at a spot in front of you. Inhale as

Exhale   Inhale   Exhale   Inhale   . . .   Exhale

you step your right foot forward into a lunge, making sure your right knee is parallel with your right ankle and that your right foot is parallel. Exhale as you press the right foot against the floor and step your left foot forward to the ready position. Inhale. Step your left leg forward to lunge, making sure your left knee is parallel with your ankle, and exhale as you step your right foot forward to the ready position. Do 12 to 15 repetitions on each side. Note: Keep your spine vertical the whole time, and keep your pelvis like the Warrior 1 position.

FOCUS ON FORM

Breath/Focus: Keep your focus in front of you and keep breathing full breaths the whole time.

Ground: You are grounding from your feet. Your legs should be hip-width apart and your feet parallel when lunging. Avoid stepping forward too far. You should easily be able to step the back leg into Ready position.

Center: Draw you tailbone under slightly to maintain a neutral position (like you do in Warrior 1 pose), and engage your core muscles to avoid arching your lower back when lunging.

Expand: Keep your breastbone lifted and shoulders relaxed, and create space in your torso for your breath to provide support.

Lengthen: You are lengthening through your spine. Make sure your spine is vertical and not leaning forward (over the front leg) when lunging.

THE RIGHT STABILITY BALL FOR YOU

When you sit on the ball, your hips and knees should be bent at a 90-degree angle.

55 cm ball for people who are 5' to 5'8"
65 cm ball for people who are 5'8" to 6'2"

Stability Bridge

Benefit: Stability bridge helps increase both your balance and your stability while developing strength in the core and back body muscles.

Muscle being strengthened: Buttocks, hamstrings, shins

Assisting: core (transverse abdominis, erector spinae), upper back muscles (trapezius, rhomboids)

Complementary strength poses: Back-bending poses such as Locust pose, Bow pose

Complementary flexibility poses: Standing and seated forward bending poses such as Standing Forward Bend pose, Back-Stretching pose

Lie on your back and place your feet on the ball with legs "glued" together; feet are flexed. Keep your arms alongside your body, palms facing down. Inhale as you lift your pelvis toward the ceiling to a bridge pose, exhale at the top, and try to hold for 5 to 10 breaths. Exhale as you roll down, vertebra by vertebra, to the starting position. Repeat 10 to 15 times.

When you feel stable and comfortable doing this exercise, add on a "pull-in." Inhale, lift up to bridge, and exhale; bend your legs to pull your heels toward your buttocks, making sure your pelvis stays lifted. Inhale, extend to bridge. Exhale, roll down, vertebra by vertebra. Repeat 10 to 15 times.

FOCUS ON FORM

Breath/Focus: Make sure you work the breath with your movements. Inhale as you lift up to bridge and exhale as you lower. On the pull-ins:

Exhale   Inhale   Exhale   Inhale   Exhale

Exhale as you pull in; inhale as you extend. Keep your focus at a spot toward the ceiling.

Ground: You might feel a little wobbly at first, but spread your fingers, keep your arms open, and press your palms and upper back into the floor to provide you with strong support. Flexing the feet will help as well.

Center: Keep your pelvis in a neutral position (draw your tailbone under) the whole time by engaging your core muscles for support.

Expand: Lift your breastbone, roll your shoulders back, and draw your shoulder blades together.

Lengthen: Feel length through your spine first and foremost. With this, you are better able to create extension through your whole body, from your heels to the crown of your head.

MACHINES

Leg Curl

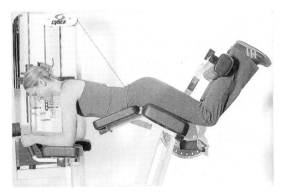

Benefit: The leg curl is an isolation exercise and will strengthen the muscles in the back of your upper leg.

Muscle being strengthened: Hamstrings

Assisting: Core muscles (transverse abdominis, erector spinae), buttocks, biceps, upper back muscles (trapezius, rhomboids)

Complementary strength poses: Backward-bending poses such as Locust pose, Bow pose

Inhale   Exhale

Complementary flexibility poses: Downward-Facing Dog pose, Back-Stretching pose

Lie on your belly and adjust your pelvis into a neutral position. Gaze at a spot on the floor. Hold onto the handlebars. Keep your breastbone lifted and engage your shoulder blades. Keep your feet flexed. Don't lose this position as you exhale and bend your legs, moving your heels toward your buttocks. Inhale as you extend (avoid hyperextending your knees). Do 12 to 15 repetitions.

FOCUS ON FORM

Breath/Focus: Exhale as you curl; inhale as you extend. Keep your gaze at a spot on the floor while being mindful of how your lower back responds to the leg curls.

Ground: You are grounding through your pelvis.

Center: Do not let your hip bones lift off the bench. Keep your tailbone drawn under and core muscles engaged to maintain a neutral pelvis. Avoid "crunching" the lower back muscles. Keeping the pelvis motionless will isolate the hamstrings more.

Expand: Keeping your breastbone lifted, shoulders relaxed, and shoulder blades together will help you create space in your rib cage to fully breathe.

Lengthen: Maintain length in your spine, from your tailbone to the crown of your head. Avoid dropping your head; keep it lifted.

Leg Extension

Benefit: The leg extension is an isolation exercise and strengthens the muscles in the front of your upper leg.

Muscles being strengthened: Quadriceps

Assisting: Core muscles (transverse abdominis), upper back muscles (trapezius, rhomboids), biceps

Complementary strength poses: The leg extension will help you isolate your quadriceps for poses such as Attention pose, one leg balancing

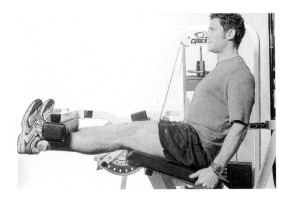

poses, and standing and seated forward bends

Complementary flexibility poses: Upward-Facing Dog pose, Half Frog pose, Bow pose

Position the back rest and leg rest to fit your body. Keep your feet flexed, hold the handlebars and keep your rib cage lifted. Gaze at a spot in front of you. Exhale as you contract your quadriceps to extend your legs (avoid hyperextending the knees) and inhale as you bend your legs (avoid bending so much that the weights touch). Do 12 to 15 repetitions.

FOCUS ON FORM

Breath/Focus: Exhale as you extend the legs; inhale as you bend the legs. Keep your focus at a spot in front of you while being aware of working your quadriceps.

Ground: You are grounding through your pelvis.

Center: Pelvis is slightly tilted forward to sit on your sitting bones. Draw your power from your core muscles.

Expand: Keep your breastbone lifted, shoulders relaxed, and shoulder blades drawn down, hold onto the handlebars and engage the biceps. Lift your rib cage out of your hips to make room for deeper breaths and better isolation of the quadriceps.

Lengthen: Keep your spine vertical and lengthened. Keep the weight at a point where you can keep your spine lengthened and avoid hunching forward.

Inhale   Exhale

CORE WORK ON THE BALL

The core exercises for Level 2 work deeper into your abdominal muscles. You might feel these a little differently in the beginning (almost like you're not working them at all), but believe me, you will feel them the next day! There is nothing superficial about these exercises. Not only will your core be sleek and strong, but it will help you move through life, providing strong physical support for any situation that comes your way. These core exercises are a great complement to the arm balancing yoga poses. I will tell you to: ABSolutely have a ball.

Stability Tail Lift

Benefit: The stability tail lift isolates the part of the abdomen that's hardest to tone up, the lower part often referred to as the belly. Being able to isolate this area is helpful in standing balancing poses and for moving into inverted poses.

Muscles being strengthened: Core muscles (transverse abdominis, rectus abdominis, obliques)

Complementary strength poses: Downward-Facing Dog pose, Fierce pose

Complementary flexibility poses: Backward-bending postures such as Upward-Facing Dog pose, Bow pose

Lie on your back with your legs lifted to the ceiling. Your arms can be behind your head or at your sides. Exhale as you try to roll your tailbone off the floor (to lift); inhale as you release without dropping it to the floor. Do 10 to 15 repetitions.

Inhale   Exhale

Breath/Focus: Exhale as you lift; inhale as you come back to the floor. Keep your focus at a spot toward the ceiling.

Ground: You are grounding through your spine.

Center: Keep the tailbone drawn under so the pelvis tilts backward. Don't use momentum here to throw your legs up in the air; you need to lift from the lower abdomen. The movement might barely be there in the beginning, but as you practice the lower abs will get stronger and you'll be able to lift higher.

Expand: A sign that you are overdoing it is when you tense your neck and crunch your shoulder. Your neck should be resting on the floor. Take your time and don't be in a rush. The height of the lift is not important in the beginning; it will come. Work on the isolation and the breath.

Lengthen: You are lengthening through your spine. Keep your head rested on the floor and feel the length in your neck.

Stability Plank and Bi-lateral Pull-In

Benefit: Stability Plank & Pull-in is designed to create strength and stability in core and upper body muscles.

Muscles being strengthened: Core muscles (transverse abdominis, rectus abdominis, erector spinae), buttocks, chest, upper back muscles (trapezius, rhomboids, latissimus dorsi), triceps.

Complementary strength postures: Plank pose, Chaturanga

Complementary flexibility postures: Upward-Facing Dog pose, Downward-Facing Dog pose

Place your feet on the ball and point your toes. Keep your arms shoulder-width apart and parallel to your shoulders. Spread your fingers and ground your palms. Feel a full extension from your toes to the crown of your head. Make sure your pelvis and head are lifted and that you feel the full extension through your body. Hold this Plank position for 3 to 5 breath cycles. Once you feel stable in this position, move onto the "pull-in."

From Stability plank exhale as you bend your legs to pull your knees toward your chest. Then inhale back to Stability plank. Do 8 to 15 repetitions.

FOCUS ON FORM

Breath/Focus: Keep your gaze at a spot on the floor. Breathe smooth and even breaths.

Ground: You are grounding through your hand/arms and tops of your feet on the ball.

Center: Keep your pelvis in a neutral position with your core muscles engaged. Avoid letting your pelvis sink, creating an arch in the lower back.

Expand: Keep breast bone lifted so you can roll your shoulders back to draw shoulder blades onto your back for upper back support.

Lengthen: Maintain extension in your spine (avoid dropping your head) whether staying in Stability plank or drawing your knees in on the pull-in.

Inhale/Exhale   Inhale   Exhale   Inhale

Stability Oblique Bend

Benefit: Stability oblique bend creates full body integration while strengthening, balancing, and stabilizing the side muscles.

Muscles being strengthened: Core (obliques, quadratus lumborum), inner thighs, outer thighs

Complementary strength poses: Triangle posture, extended side lateral bend, Side Plank pose

Complementary flexibility poses: Seated and standing twists such as Twisted Fierce pose, Revolved Triangle pose

Move close to a wall. Place the right side of your body over the ball with your feet placed against the wall supporting you. Place your right hand on your left hip and your left hand behind your head. You'll start out feeling a stretch in your hip and side ribs. Exhale as you lift up as if you are extending your body sideways, while contracting your left oblique muscle. Then inhale as you lower back into the starting position. Do 12 to 15 repetitions.

FOCUS ON FORM

Breath/Focus: Exhale as you lift, inhale as you lower. Keep the breath smooth as you bend.

Ground: You are grounding through both your feet and your pelvis.

Center: Keep your pelvis in a neutral position and engage your core muscles. Make sure you don't rotate your pelvis when you bend. Bend sideways from the bottom of your left rib.

Expand: Your breastbone stays lifted, and your shoulders stay relaxed. Avoid using your leg muscles to lift.

Inhale   Exhale

Lengthen: You are lengthening through your spine first and foremost. You are creating extension from your feet to the crown of your head.

UPPER BODY—CHEST

These upper body exercises will help you gain strength and stability. They will also add tone and definition to your upper body. These exercises complement the arm balancing yoga poses and inversions, enabling you to balance and breathe even when you're balancing on your arms or turning upside down.

Flat Bench Chest Fly

Benefit: This chest fly is designed to isolate, tone, lift, and strengthen your chest muscles.

Muscles being strengthened: Chest muscles

Assisting: Biceps muscles, core muscles

Complementary strength poses: Plank pose, Chaturanga

Complementary flexibility poses: Backward-bending poses such as Bow pose, Upward-Facing Dog pose

Lie on a bench with your legs bent and your feet on the bench, with your legs together and your spine supported. Hold a pair of dumbbells in your hands. Keep your arms extended and shoulder width apart, palms facing each other. With a slight bend in the elbows, inhale as you open your arms to the side, drawing your shoulder blades together. You should feel a stretch through your chest. Exhale

Inhale   Exhale

and contract the outer part of your chest as you draw your palms together without the weights touching. This should feel as if you are hugging a big person. Do 12 to 15 repetitions.

FOCUS ON FORM

Breath/Focus: Focus at a spot on the ceiling. Inhale as you open, exhale as you close.

Ground: You are grounding through your spine and your feet.

Center: Draw your tailbone under slightly to engage your core muscles and avoid arching your lower back while working the chest muscles.

Expand: Keep your breastbone lifted and shoulders relaxed, expanding your rib cage and creating more space for your breath. This also allows you to isolate the chest muscles.

Lengthen: Maintain the length in your spine throughout the exercise.

UPPER BODY—BACK

Seated Cable Row

Benefit: The seated cable row is designed to improve your posture by strengthening the muscles in your upper back.

Muscles being strengthened: Upper back muscles (latissimus dorsi, teres major, rhomboids, trapezius), shoulders (posterior deltoid), biceps

Inhale   Exhale

Assisting: Core muscles

Complementary strength poses: Stick pose, Plank pose

Complementary flexibility poses: Standing and seated twists such as Twisted Fierce pose, Marichyasana C

Place your feet on the board with your legs bent and about shoulder-width apart. Bend forward from your hips. Grasp the handlebar with both hands. Pull the handlebar back and sit tall. Exhale as you contract your shoulder blades and pull your elbows back (this is a continuous exhale). Then inhale as you slowly extend the arms. Do 12 to 15 repetitions.

FOCUS ON FORM

Breath/Focus: Keep your focus at a spot in front of you. Exhale as you pull your arms back; inhale as you extend your arms.

Ground: You are grounding through your pelvis.

Center: Allow the tailbone to move backwards a little to maintain a slight anterior tilt in the pelvis. Sit at the top of your sitting bones. This will help you to engage your core muscles and create expansion through your torso.

Expand: Keep your breastbone lifted and your shoulders relaxed. Draw your shoulder blades into your back for upper back support. Your torso should not move as you move your arms.

Lengthen: Keep the length in your spine throughout the exercise.

UPPER BODY—SHOULDERS

Shoulder Press

Benefit: The shoulder press is designed to give your shoulders shape and strength.

Muscles being strengthened: Middle (medial) shoulders, upper back (upper trapezius, serratus anterior), triceps

Complementary strength poses: Arm balancing poses such as Downward-Facing Dog pose.

Complementary flexibility poses: Arm Reaching pose, Fierce pose

From the ready position, hold your elbows at your sides and the dumbbells at shoulder level. Exhale as you push the dumbbells above your head without hyperextending your arms. Inhale as you return your elbows to shoulder level.

Make sure that you don't arch your back or round your upper spine. Keep your pelvis neutral and your abdomen active. As you push the dumbbells up think of pulling your shoulders down. This will ensure that you will keep some space between your shoulders and your ears. Keep your wrists firm and do not hyperextend the arms. Do 12 to 15 repetitions.

FOCUS ON FORM

Breath/Focus: Keep your focus at a spot in front of you. Exhale as you lift; inhale as you lower.

Ground: You are grounding through your feet.

Center: Keep your pelvis in a neutral position; engage your core muscles and make sure that your pelvis is not affected by extending your arms.

Expand: Keep your breastbone lifted and your shoulders away from your ears. Think of drawing your shoulder blades down and together when you work the arms.

Lengthen: You are lengthening through your spine.

Inhale

Exhale

Dumbbell Side Lateral Raise

Benefit: The side lateral raise is designed to tone and strengthen the outer part of your shoulders.

Muscles being strengthened: Mostly the middle part of the shoulders, but also front and back parts of the shoulder

Complementary strength poses: Side Plank, Warrior 2

Complementary flexibility poses: Eagle pose

In the ready position, keep your arms at your sides with the elbows slightly bent. Exhale as you lift the dumbbells to shoulder height. Inhale as you return your arms to your sides without touching your body. Do 12 to 15 repetitions.

FOCUS ON FORM

Breath/Focus: Exhale as you lift; inhale as you lower.

Ground: You are grounding through your legs. Make sure your feet are parallel.

Center: As you lift the dumbbells, keep your pelvis firmly held in a neutral position and engage your core muscles.

Expand: Keep your breastbone lifted, your shoulders relaxed, and your shoulder blades contracted for upper back support.

Lengthen: You are lengthening through your spine. Avoid throwing your head back. If your neck feels strained, you're lifting too much weight.

Inhale

Exhale

Dumbbell Horizontal Shoulder Internal Rotation

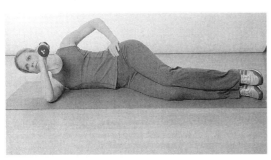

Benefit: The dumbbell horizontal shoulder internal rotation strengthens your rotator cuff and provides support for your shoulders.

Muscles being strengthened: Rotator cuff; subscapularis

Complementary strength poses: Inversions, arm balances

Complementary flexibility poses: Twisting and binding poses such as Marichyasana A and C, Extended Side Angle pose (binding in front)

Lie on your side with your legs bent. Your head must be in a neutral position. If it is uncomfortable to keep it lifted, rest it on a pillow, or a folded towel. Hold a dumbbell horizontally in your bottom hand at a 90-degree angle. Rest your top arm on your waist. (In order to target your rotator cuffs, go lighter on the weight. Use a 3 to 5 pound weight.)

Contract the internal rotator as you exhale and rotate the lower arm up to a 90-degree angle (vertical). Then inhale and return to the horizontal position. Do 15 to 20 repetitions.

FOCUS ON FORM

Breath/Focus: Exhale to the vertical position. Inhale back to the horizontal position.

Inhale   Exhale

Ground: You are grounding through the whole right side of your body.

Center: Keep your pelvis in a neutral position, engaging your core muscles and making sure that the lower arm is the only part of the body that is moving.

Expand: Keep your rib cage lifted in order to breathe in this position.

Lengthen: You are lengthening through your spine.

Dumbbell seated shoulder external rotation

Benefit: The dumbbell seated shoulder external rotation is designed to strengthen your rotator cuff and helps provide support for your shoulders.

Muscles being strengthened: Rotator cuff: infraspinatus, teres minor

Complementary strength poses: Inversions and arm balances, Downward-Facing Dog pose

Complementary flexibility poses: Marichyasana A and C, Extended Side Angle pose (binding in front)

Sit on a chair or bench. Place your arms parallel to the floor. Keep your elbows slightly in front of and below your shoulders. Contract the external rotator and exhale as you rotate the lower arm up to a 90-

Exhale

Inhale

degree angle or as close to that as it will go. Inhale as you return. Do not rotate 90 degrees or let the elbows move. A partner can hold and support your elbows to make sure they don't move. Do 15 to 20 repetitions. (In order to target the rotater cuffs, go lighter on the weight. Use a 3 to 5 pound weight.)

FOCUS ON FORM

Breath/Focus: Exhale to end the position; inhale to start the position. Gaze at a spot in front of you.

Ground: You are grounding through your pelvis.

Center: Allow the tailbone to move backwards a little to maintain a slight anterior tilt in the pelvis. Sit at the top of your sitting bones; this helps you engage your core muscles and creates expansion through your torso.

Expand: Keeping your breastbone lifted and your shoulders relaxed will help you better isolate your rotator cuff muscles.

Lengthen: You are lengthening through your spine.

BICEPS

Biceps Curl

Benefit: The biceps curl strengthens and tones the muscles in the front of your arms.

Muscles being strengthened: Biceps, forearms, wrists

Complementary strength poses: Downward-Facing Dog pose, Plank pose, Chaturanga

Complementary flexibility poses: Twisting postures such as Marichyasana C and Revolved Triangle pose

From the ready position, keep your arms at your sides with your palms facing your outer thighs.

Exhale as you rotate your palms to face your body and bend your elbows. Inhale as you return your arms to your sides. Make sure your elbows do not flare to the side. Do 12 to 15 repetitions.

FOCUS ON FORM

Breath/Focus: Keep the breath steady and even with the movement. Your focus is at a spot in front of you.

Ground: You are grounding through your feet.

Center: Keep your pelvis in a neutral position with your core muscles engaged for support.

Expand: Your breastbone is lifted, shoulders relaxed, and shoulder blades pulled together for upper back support.

Lengthen: You are lengthening throughout your spine.

Inhale

Exhale

TRICEPS

Supine Triceps Extension

Benefit: Supine triceps extension strengthens and tones the muscles in the back of your arm.

Muscles being strengthened: Triceps

Complementary strength poses: Upward-Facing Dog pose, Plank pose, Side Plank pose, Chaturanga

Complementary flexibility poses: Cow's Face pose

Lie on your back with your legs bent. With dumbbells in your hands, extend your arms to a vertical position. Keep your arms shoulder-width apart. Inhale, bend at the elbows, and lower the weight toward

your ears. Exhale and extend your arms back to the vertical position. Your elbows should not move. Do 12 to 15 repetitions.

FOCUS ON FORM

Breath/Focus: Breath should be steady the whole time. Inhale, bend arms; exhale, extend arms. Keep your focus toward the ceiling.

Ground: You are grounding through your back body.

Center: Draw your tailbone under slightly to keep your pelvis in a neutral position. Engage your core muscles.

Expand: Keep your breastbone lifted and your shoulders relaxed and draw your shoulder blades together. This will help you to stabilize your arms and avoid moving your elbows back and forth.

Lengthen: Keep the spine lengthened throughout the entire exercise.

Exhale

Inhale

Level 2 Endurance

AEROBIC ENDURANCE ACTIVITIES

4-week Power Walking program

WEEK	PROGRAM	MINUTES	INTENSITY
1	Warm-up phase	3–5	40–50 %
	Target heart rate phase: flat	20–25	60 %
	Warm-down phase	3–5	Resting heart rate + 10 points
2	Warm-up phase	3–5	40–50 %
	Target heart rate phase: flat/hilly	25	55–65 %
	Warm-down phase	3–5	Resting heart rate + 10 points
3	Warm-up phase	3–5	40–50 %
	Target heart rate phase: flat/very hilly/flat	20–25	55–65 %
	Warm-down phase	3–5	Resting heart rate + 10 points
4	Warm-up phase	3–5	40–50 %
	Target heart rate phase: flat/hilly/very hilly/flat	25	60–70 %
	Warm-down phase	3–5	Resting heart rate + 10 points

4-Week Biking Program

WEEK	PROGRAM	MINUTES	INTENSITY
1	Warm-up phase	3–5	40–50 %
	Target heart rate phase: flat	20–25	50–60 %
	Warm-down phase	3–5	Resting heart rate + 10 points
2	Warm-up phase	3–5	40–50 %
	Target heart rate phase: flat/hilly	25	50–60 %
	Warm-down phase	3–5	Resting heart rate + 10 points
3	Warm-up phase	3–5	40–50 %
	Target heart rate phase: flat/very hilly/flat	20–25	60 %
	Warm-down phase	3–5	Resting heart rate + 10 points
4	Warm-up phase	3–5	40–50 %
	Target heart rate phase: flat/hilly/very hilly/flat	25	60–70 %
	Warm-down phase	3–5	Resting heart rate + 10 points

You can use this program both indoors on a treadmill or outside on the road. There is a difference between running outside on the road and running inside on a treadmill. Just because you run well on a treadmill doesn't mean it will be smooth sailing outside. The tread-mill tends to speed you along; you get a lot of help and can get away with a lot. Outside there isn't much help—it's just you, your body, and the road. Everything gets put to the test, so you should change it up and alternate the two.

Running is a very one-dimensional sport with one directional movement; it's easy to overuse muscles. Because of its higher impact, the pounding of running has a tendency to tighten the mus-cles of the lower body, such as the hip flexors, hamstrings, outer thighs, inner thighs, and feet.

Supportive conditioning exercises

These muscles often get overtaxed and need flexibility: Feet, plantar arch-es and ankles, calves, hamstrings, adductors, buttocks, hip flexors, lower back, shoulders, neck

These muscles are often underutilized and need strengthening: Back muscles, arms, rotator cuffs, core

The leg muscles of course need strength (together with flexibility), but the upper body needs strength as well to prevent hunching forward and to provide support for the lower body.

Running Posture and Technique

Just as in walking, your body is your tool when you run, so it's important you match your physical body posture to your running posture and technique. The posture in running is erect, but dynam-ic. The yoga category you can most draw on for running is the standing balancing poses. In these poses, just as in running, you are grounding through your feet, centering through your pelvis and core, lengthening through your spine, and expanding through your rib cage.

Running is like a flow/vinyasa—connect the breath with movement. Make sure you avoid hunching the upper body. If the upper back muscles are too flexible and the chest muscles have become tight, your shoulders and neck will be tight too and will have a negative effect on your lower back and hamstrings. The stronger your upper body, the more your legs can work. A combination of strength and flexibility in your legs will help your upper body relax and elongate. With a strong core to connect both, they will work together in unison.

Lower Body

It's important you run with lightness, which will put a spring in your step. Avoid running with a "clonk." This might mean that you are overstriding and locking your knees (not a good thing).

Running with lightness is important for a very good reason. For every mile you run your foot will be in contact with the ground about one thousand times. The impact on each foot is about four times your body weight. The principle of lightness from yoga can help you minimize the pounding your feet go through during running.

It's important you use your whole foot; from the heel, to the forefoot, to the toes so you hit the pavement evenly with your feet. As you leave the ground give a little push with your big toe.

To get more bounce and lightness in your running try to flex your ankle during the run. This happens naturally when you roll from the heels, to the forefoot, to the toes as described above. Using the recommended yoga poses will stretch and strengthen your ankles. The less rigid they are, the more lightness you can create.

Lift your knees; this will help you cover more ground and put spring in your step. Never lock your knees; always keep them slightly bent.

Core

Because of the constant forward motion in running, the hamstrings and hip flexors get very tight. This can pull on the lower back muscles, cause the pelvis to tilt forward, and result in a swayback.

A swayback will make it hard to create length in your spine, and will inhibit the flow of energy. Being aware of your core strength and flexibility will make you think about the position of your pelvis, so you can adjust it when it moves out of alignment. Give the pelvis room to move with your stride; don't lock it into a fixed position.

Upper Body and Arms

In two-legged locomotion, the upper body plays an integral role. The arms contribute to the driving force and the entire upper body helps to counterbalance the leg action.

You are lengthening from your pelvis to the crown of your head. Your spine must be perpendicular to the ground. Keeping this erect posture will free your legs to do their work and create more room for breathing.

Shoulders/Back/Chest

You need to keep your upper body engaged, yet relaxed, and for that you need a balance of strength and flexibility in your upper body. If you are aligned from the ground up, it will be easier to relax your shoulders. Draw the shoulder blades down and slightly together and keep the breastbone lifted to ensure a relaxed shoulder position. This allows you to create more space between your rib cage and your hips. Your breath can move to your lower back and increase air flow, allowing the lungs to do their work. You will move more freely with an open rib cage and your legs will perform better.

Arms/Elbows/Hands

The arms and legs must work together in rhythm; the elbows should be unlocked. The faster you run, the more your arms must be part of the action. The slower you run, the less they need to be involved. Each arm should swing across the chest, without passing the midline.

The more you clench your hands, the more tension builds in your arms and shoulders. So keep your hands unclenched; think of the way you hold a dumbbell without clenching it.

Neck/Head

By putting the alignment principles of grounding, centering, expanding, and lengthening into action, your neck and head will be in a better position. Be light and balanced as you run tall and look forward. Enjoy the amazing view!

Keep the neck long. If your upper back muscles are strong you will naturally lengthen your neck and keep your head in the right position. But if your upper body muscles are weak and you end up hunching forward, this will have a negative effect on your head and neck.

The Warm-Up

Incorporating the Sun Salutations is very helpful because they give your upper body strength and stretch your feet, ankles, legs, hip flexors, shoulders, chest, and spine. This prevents shin splints and helps your feet. Rolling over the toes in the complementary Chaturanga (yoga push-up) to Upward-Facing Dog and to Downward-Facing Dog increases circulation and also balances the calf and shin muscles.

The Warm-Down

Forward bending and backward bending poses balance and strengthen the muscles of the front body and back body. Twisting postures are important, too, for hip and spinal flexibility. The inverted postures work your cardiovascular system in a different way, and also create lightness and take weight off of your feet. Core strength is important to provide support for the lower back muscles.

Focus

Your focus is in front of you toward the road. If you are on a treadmill, focus on a spot in front of you, visualizing yourself running on a road.

Flow and Energy

Running is really a perfect sport in which to put all the yoga principle of flow into action—energy, circulation, expansion, grounding, lengthening and breathing with movement. When your body is in the right position you will experience a feeling of freedom and lightness while running.

Make sure you breathe fully when you run. It is hard to incorporate proper breathing when you are running. To breathe properly, you must move toward correct body alignment in your running. Otherwise, it will be hard for energy to flow through your body.

Safety, Caution, and Rest

Investing in good running shoes, periodically changing the surface you run on, alternating indoor and outdoor running, and cross-training with the elliptical machine and stairmaster help prevent injury.

You can effectively cross-train by exercising in a way that mimics the movements of running (the elliptical machine, stairmaster, or "running" in a pool).

4-week Running Program

WEEK	PROGRAM	MINUTES	INTENSITY
1	Warm-up phase	3–5	50 %
	Target heart rate phase: flat	25–30	60–70 %
	Warm-down phase	3–5	Resting heart rate + 10 points
2	Warm-up phase	3–5	40–50 %
	Target heart rate phase: flat/hilly	25	60 %
	Warm-down phase	3–5	Resting heart rate + 10 points
3	Warm-up phase	3–5	40–50 %
	Target heart rate phase: flat/very hilly/flat	20–25	60–70 %
	Warm-down phase	3–5	Resting heart rate + 10 points
4	Warm-up phase	3–5	40–50 %
	Target heart rate phase: flat/hilly/very hilly/flat	25	60 %
	Warm-down phase	3–5	Resting heart rate + 10 points

The elliptical machine is a combination of the stairmaster and the treadmill. The legs and feet move in a long gliding motion. You can change the resistance and go backward as well as forward. The machine provides you with extra leg work at a lower impact than running; it can be a nice change for the muscles. The movement, however, is very confined to the machine.

Supportive Conditioning Exercises

These muscles are often overtaxed and need flexibility: Feet, ankles, hip flexors, shoulders, neck, lower back, calves, hamstrings, quadriceps

These muscles are often underutilized and need strength: Upper back muscles, lower back, core, arms, shoulders

Elliptical Posture and Technique

The posture for the elliptical machine is much the same as for running, but this activity is more stationary. The machine provides a low-impact, high-intensity workout for the lower body.

Using an elliptical machine is similar to holding the standing balancing postures for several breaths. You are stationary, but at the same time you are moving because you are adapting your physical body to the activity in which you are involved. You are constantly being tested in fitting your posture to the machine.

You are grounding through your feet, centering through your pelvis and core, expanding through your rib cage, and lengthening through your spine.

Avoid hunching and relying too much on the rails to support you. Use your own support system, your skeleton. Avoid "cranking up the volume" if you can't support it and end up hunching. By slowing down the pace and not holding onto the handlebars, you'll have to balance more and use your core strength.

A hunched posture will make the upper back muscles too flexible and the chest muscles too tight; it will also make it harder to breathe and to get the energy to flow through your body. It also results in tight shoulders and a tight neck, and it will have a negative impact on the lower back and hamstrings.

4-week Elliptical Program

WEEK	PROGRAM	MINUTES	INTENSITY
1	Warm-up phase	3–5	50 %
	Target heart rate phase: flat	25–30	60–70 %
	Warm-down phase	3–5	Resting heart rate + 10 points
2	Warm-up phase	3–5	40–50 %
	Target heart rate phase: flat/hilly	25	60–70 %
	Warm-down phase	3–5	Resting heart rate + 10 points
3	Warm-up phase	3–5	40–50 %
	Target heart rate phase: flat/very hilly/flat	20–25	60–70 %
	Warm-down phase	3–5	Resting heart rate + 10 points
4	Warm-up phase	3–5	40–50 %
	Target heart rate phase: flat/hilly/very hilly/flat	25	60 %
	Warm-down phase	3–5	Resting heart rate + 10 points

The stronger your upper body is, the more your legs can work. A combination of strength and flexibility in your legs helps your upper body relax. A strong core bridges the upper body and lower body, allowing them to work together in unison.

Lower Body

It's important to place your feet parallel on the platforms with your toes spread. Elliptical platforms provide plenty of foot space.

Keep your feet parallel and press back through your heels so that you can use the back thigh muscles (glutes and hamstrings). Don't hyperextend the knee. Contract your quad muscles as you press down. You should feel the alternate "push and pull" action in your muscles and it should feel like you are working both legs evenly.

Core

Just as In running, your pelvis should be in a neutral position with room to move. Use the core muscles to provide stability and support to the pelvis and lower back. This will also keep you from arching your lower back.

Upper Body

Keep your shoulders relaxed, with your shoulder blades drawn down and slightly together, and your breastbone lifted. Try not to hold the rails; if you do, hold them lightly. This will force you to use your balance and core muscles. Your arms are bent but relaxed at your sides. Test your balance by trying not to hold onto the handlebars. Intensity should be such that you don't have to hold them.

The Warm-Up

Incorporating the Sun Salutations is very helpful because they give your upper body strength and stretch your feet, ankles, legs, hip flexors, shoulders, chest, and spine. This prevents shin splints and is very user-friendly for your feet. Rolling over the toes from Chaturanga to Upward-Facing Dog and to Downward-Facing Dog increases the circulation in your feet and helps balance the calf and shin muscles by alternately stretching and strengthening them (Downward-Facing Dog stretches the calf and strengthens the shin, and Upward-Facing Dog stretches the shin and strengthens the calf).

The Warm-Down

It's important to do both forward bending and backward bending poses to balance and strengthen the muscles of the front body and back body. Twists are important, too, for hip and spinal flexibility. These also improve your core strength.

Focus

Try not to distract yourself by reading a magazine or looking at the TV screen. Find a spot in front of you where you can focus and pay attention to your alignment during the activity. Count your breaths and steps and visualize yourself stepping to the top of the Empire State Building.

Flow and Energy

Try to coordinate your breathing with your movement. Deep diaphragmatic breathing is recommended. Keeping the shoulders relaxed while maintaining length in your spine and working at a tempo you can physically support makes it easier to breathe deep and increases your energy expenditure. Hanging over the rails is a sign that the intensity is too high. Slow down and stand erect. You'll burn more calories, you'll look better, and you will feel amazing! Your movement throughout this activity should feel connected and light.

Safety, Caution, and Rest

Don't go faster than your body can handle. Get used to the machine before you "crank up the volume."

CHAPTER 5

Welcome to Level 3

Level 3 is where you should start if:

▲ You have successfully completed Level 2

▲ You are already working out and know and perform all of the yoga postures and strength-training exercises in Level 2

▲ You want to learn how to continue integrating the three elements of physical fitness into a balanced program for optimal conditioning

This third level of the Goa System will help you build a solid tower of flexibility, strength, and endurance.

▲ Yoga flexibility postures are added to further challenge your flexibility, balance, and strength. In this level you continue to practice the ribcage breathing from Level 2 and together with the yoga postures increase your flexibility and expand your breath. You also learn another balancing pose.

▲ Strength-training exercises for this level work more with single-side stabilization and challenge your weaker side. Other strength-training exercises will increase your strength and stability, particular for your upper body. The stability ball exercises work with single-side stabilization as well, which increases your core strength and helps you balance better.

▲ The Level 3 aerobic exercises further increase your endurance by increasing your time and intensity. You can continue with power walking, biking, running, aerobic dance, or step aerobics from Level 2; or, choose new activities such as the stairmaster and spinning classes.

For the Level 3 program, plan to do four to five 75 to 90 minute workouts per week. The charts below provide guidelines on which exercises to do for how long. Follow the 4-week program structure provided for this level; within the general guidelines you can adjust each activity to an intensity and duration level that works for you and your lifestyle.

Yoga Flexibility Program

(from Levels 1 and 2)

YOGA POSTURE CATEGORY	YOGA POSTURE	REPS EACH SIDE /BREATH CYCLES/ TOTAL APPROX. TIME
Warm-Up/Warm-Down		
	Sun Salutation A Sun Salutation B	2 reps of each sun salutation/$^1/_2$ breath cycle for each yoga posture, except 3–5 breath cycles in Downward-Facing Dog/5 minutes
Standing Balancing		
On both feet	*Warrior 2*	1 rep/5 breath cycles/1 minute
Side lateral bend	*Extended side angle*	1 rep/5 breath cycles/1 minute
	Triangle pose	1 rep/5 breath cycles/1 minute
Twist	Rotated Triangle pose	1 rep/5 breath cycles/1 minute
	Twisted Fierce pose	1 rep/5 breath cycles/1 minute
On one foot	*Extended Hand to Big Toe*	1 rep/5 breath cycles/1 minute
	Warrior 3	1 rep/5 breath cycles/1 minute

(Continued)

Yoga Flexibility Program
(from Levels 1 and 2) (*Continued*)

YOGA POSTURE CATEGORY	YOGA POSTURE	REPS EACH SIDE /BREATH CYCLES/ TOTAL APPROX. TIME
	Eagle pose	1 rep/5 breath cycles/1 minute
	Tree pose	1 rep/5 breath cycles/1 minute
Arm Balancing	*Hand stand*	
	Side plank	1 rep/5 breath cycles/1 minute
	Crow pose	1 rep/5 breath cycles/1 minute
Seated	Stick pose	1 rep/5 breath cycles/1 minute
Forward bending	*Marichyasana A*	1 rep/5 breath cycles/2 minutes
	Back-stretching pose	1 rep/5 breath cycles/30 seconds
	Bound Angle pose	1 rep/5 breath cycles/30 seconds
	Cow's Face pose/ Child's pose	1 rep/5 breath cycles/2 minutes
Twist	Marichyasana C	1 rep/5 breath cycles/1 minute
Backward bending	*Pigeon Quad stretch*	1 rep/5 breath cycles/2 minutes
	Wheel	2–3 reps/5 breath cycles/2 minutes
	Bow pose	1–2 reps/5 breath cycles/1 minute
	Fish pose	1 rep/5 breath cycles/30 seconds
	Shoulder stand	1 rep/15–25 breath cycles/2–4 minutes
Relaxation	Savasana	5 minutes

Strength-Training Program

EQUIPMENT	BODY PART	EXERCISE	SETS/REPS/TOTAL APPROX. TIME
Body weight	Legs	Single leg squat	2 sets/12–15 reps/4 minutes
Dumbbells		Walking lunges	2 sets/12–15 reps/4 minutes
Machine		Single leg press	2 sets/12–15 reps/4 minutes
		Leg press	1 set/12–15 reps/1 minute
		Single leg extension	2 sets/12–15 reps/4 minutes
		Leg extension	1 set/12–15 reps/1 minute
		Single leg curl	2 sets/12–15 reps/4 minutes
		Leg curl	1 set/12–15 reps/1 minute
Stability Ball	Core	Stability Plank/Unilateral stability pull-in	1–2 sets/12–15 reps/2 minutes
		Bilateral stability pull-in	1–2 sets/12–15 reps/2 minutes
		Stability back extension	2 sets/12–15 reps/2 minutes
		Stability tail lift	2 sets/12–15 reps/2 minutes
		Stability oblique bend	2 sets/12–15 reps/2 minutes
Dumbbells	Shoulders	Single shoulder press on one leg	2 sets/12–15 reps/2 minutes
		Shoulder press	1 set/12–15 reps/30 seconds
		Side lateral raise	2 sets/12–15 reps/1 minute
Barbell	Chest	Flat bench chest press	2–3 sets/12–15 reps/3 minutes
Dumbbells		Chest fly	2–3 sets/12–15 reps/3 minutes

(*Continued*)

Strength-Training Program
(Continued)

EQUIPMENT	BODY PART	EXERCISE	SETS/REPS/TOTAL APPROX. TIME
Gravitron	Back	Assisted wide pull-ups	2–3 sets/12–15 reps/3 minutes
Machine		Seated row	2–3 sets/12–15 reps/3 minutes
	Biceps	Assisted bicep pull-ups	2–3 sets/12–15 reps/3 minutes
Dumbbells		Biceps curl	2–3 sets/12–15 reps/3 minutes
	Triceps	Assisted triceps dips	2–3 sets/12–15 reps/3 minutes
Dumbbells		Supine triceps extension	2–3 sets/12–15 reps/3 minutes

Endurance Program

EXERCISE	TIME
Stairmaster	30–45 minutes
Spinning class	45 minutes
Power walk/run	30–45 minutes
Biking	30–45 minutes
Running	30–45 minutes

The 4-Week Program Structure

Day	1	2	3	4	5
Structure/ Flow	Cardio, legs, chest, back, core, yoga	Cardio, shoulders, biceps, triceps, core, yoga	Yoga day	Cardio, legs, chest, back, core, yoga	Cardio, shoulders, biceps, triceps, core, yoga
Cardio	Your choice	Your choice		Your choice	Your choice
Yoga Flexibility					
	Sun Salutation A	Sun Salutation A	Sun Salutation A	Sun Salutation A	Sun Salutation A
	Sun Salutation B	Sun Salutation B	Sun Salutation B	Sun Salutation B	Sun Salutation B
			Triangle pose	Side Plank pose	
			Rotated Triangle pose		
			Warrior 2		
			Extended side angle		
			Twisted Fierce pose		
			Crow		
			Extended Hand to Big Toe pose		
Strength			Warrior 3		

(Continued)

The 4-Week Program Structure *(Continued)*

Day	1	2	3	4	5
	Single leg press	Single shoulder press on one leg	Hand stand	Single leg squat	Single shoulder press on one leg
	Leg press	Shoulder press	Stick pose	Walking lunges	Shoulder press
		Side lateral press	Back-Stretching pose	Stability bridge	Side lateral raise
			Bound Angle pose		
	Single leg extension	Horizontal shoulder internal rotation	Cow's Face pose	Single leg extension	Horizontal shoulder internal rotation
			Marichyasana A and C		
			Pigeon quad stretch		
	Leg extension	Seated shoulder external rotation	Locust pose	Leg extension	Seated shoulder external rotation
			Bow pose		
	Single leg curl	Assisted biceps pull-ups	Wheel pose	Single leg curl	Assisted biceps pull-ups
	Leg curl	Assisted triceps dips	Back-Stretching pose	Leg curl	Assisted triceps dips

(Continued)

The 4-Week Program Structure (Continued)

Day	1	2	3	4	5
	Flat bench press		Shoulder stand		
	Assisted wide pull-ups		Fish pose		
Core	Stability tail lift	Basic crunch		Stability tail lift	Basic crunch
	Stability plank	Stability oblique bend	Child's pose	Stability plank	Stability oblique bend
	Unilateral stability pull-in	Stability back extension	Savasana	Unilateral stability pull-in	Stability back extension
Yoga Flexibility	Reclined Extended Hand to Big Toe pose	Back-Stretching pose		Reclined Extended Hand to Big Toe pose	Back-Stretching pose
	Marichyasana C	Cow's Face pose		Marichyasana C	Cow's Face pose
	Pigeon quad stretch	Marichyasana A		Pigeon quad stretch	Marichyasana A
	Locust	Marichyasana C		Locust pose	Marichyasana C
	Bow pose	Half Frog pose		Bow pose	Half Frog pose
	Wheel pose	Locust pose		Wheel pose	Locust pose
	Back-Stretching pose	Bow pose		Back-Stretching pose	Bow pose
	Savasana	Savasana		Savasana	Savasana

LEVEL 3 Yoga

THE SUN SALUTATIONS

SUN SALUTATIONS A AND B

At this point you know the Sun Salutation A and B inside out, right? You've developed upper body strength, core strength, and full body integration. This strength and integration will enable you to take the "salutation" to a deeper but lighter level. Now, instead of stepping back into Plank Pose and stepping forward from Downward-Facing Dog pose, you will learn to jump back and jump forward. This creates lightness in the body. Jumping back and jumping forward applies to both Sun Salutation A and Sun Salutation B.

You should not progress to this jumping action if you have lower back, knee, ankle, shoulder, elbow, or wrist problems.

Jump back

From the Halfway pose, gaze forward while bending at your knees and hips to shift your weight into your arms. Push firmly into the ground as you exhale to lift your hips and legs up into the air to jump into the Plank pose (legs can be extended or bent). Inhale in the Plank pose, exhale to Chaturanga, inhale to the Upward-Facing Dog pose, exhale to the Downward-Facing Dog pose.

Breath/Focus: Gaze forward at a spot on the floor in front of you. Exhale to take the jump. Inhale into Plank pose.

Ground: You are grounding through your hands. Be sure to keep arms shoulder-width apart, fingers spread, palms grounded, and arms straight.

Exhale   Inhale   Exhale   Inhale   Exhale   Inhale   Exhale   Inhale   Exhale

Center: Feel a lift through your belly to create lightness in your body and keep your core muscles active to protect your lower back when landing into Plank pose.

Expand: Keep breastbone lifted, shoulders rolled back, draw shoulder blades into your back.

Lengthen: Lengthen through your spine.

Jump forward

From Downward-Facing Dog pose, bend your knees, gaze forward between the hands as you shift your weight into the balls of your feet and hands. Lift your hips up, exhale and be ready to push off from the balls of your feet to lift the hips high into the air. Land between your hands. It might take some time before you are able to jump all the way to the hands, but the more you practice on getting lift in your hips, the further forward you will get.

Breath/Focus: Gaze at a spot between your hands. Exhale to take the jump and at the bottom of the exhalation, you should have landed between your hands.

Ground: You are grounding through your hands. Be sure to keep arms shoulder-width apart, fingers spread, palms grounded, and arms straight.

Center: Feel a lift through your belly to create lightness in your body.

Expand: Keep breastbone lifted, shoulders rolled back, draw shoulder blades into your back.

Lengthen: Lengthen your spine.

Exhale/Inhale   Exhale   Inhale   Exhale   Inhale   Exhale

Let me show you how you'll integrate Jump Forward and Jump Back into Sun Salutation B:

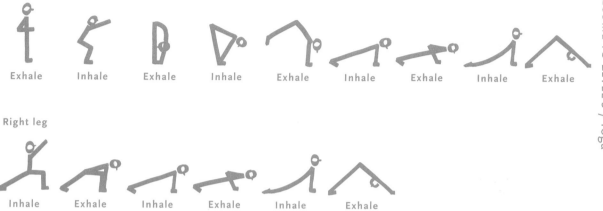

Exhale   Inhale   Exhale   Inhale   Exhale   Inhale   Exhale   Inhale   Exhale

Right leg

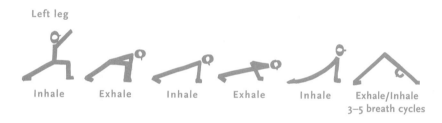

Inhale   Exhale   Inhale   Exhale   Inhale   Exhale

Left leg

Inhale   Exhale   Inhale   Exhale   Inhale   Exhale/Inhale
3–5 breath cycles

Exhale   Inhale   Exhale   Inhale   Exhale

Warrior 2

Benefit: This is primarily a strength pose. Much like Warrior 1, it creates strength in your core and lower body muscles, your shoulders and arms, and throughout your spine. Warrior 2 also stimulates the abdominal organs, diaphragm, and heart and helps expand and deepen your breath. It clears your mind and calms your brain. Warrior 2 will bring out your determination.

Warrior 2 strengthens: Quadriceps, hamstrings, buttocks, calf, shoulders (front/middle), upper back (trapezius), core (transverse abdominis), spine (lower, middle, upper)

Warrior 2 stretches: Hip flexors, inner thigh, chest, upper back (latissimus dorsi), shoulders (anterior)

Complementary strength exercises: Leg press, leg extension, leg curl, lunge, walking longer

Complementary yoga postures: Warrior 1

From Warrior 1 position square your hips and chest to the left side wall. Extend your arms to shoulder height, palms facing the floor. Reach evenly through your arms to each side of your shoulders. Turn your head to face right and focus on your right middle fingers. Stay in the pose for 5 breath cycles. Inhale into Warrior 1; exhale to Attention pose. Repeat using the left side.

FOCUS ON FORM

Breath/Focus: Gaze at your right middle fingers. Feel grounded through the legs, but light and expansive in your torso. Stretch the breath to all parts of your body.

Ground: You are grounding from the feet. All 10 toes are spread. Make sure you evenly distribute your weight in both of your legs.

Center: Adjust your pelvis to a neutral position and feel the length in your lower spine. Keep your core muscles active. Be aware of the angle of the right knee. Do not allow it to rotate to the left as you adjust your pelvis.

Inhale   Exhale   Inhale   Exhale

Expand: Relax and "drop" your shoulders. Lift your breastbone and draw your shoulder blades into your upper back.

Lengthen: Your spine is vertical. Lengthen from your pelvis to the crown of your head, and from your shoulders to your fingertips. It should feel as if someone is pulling both of your arms in opposite directions.

Extended Side Angle pose

Benefit: Extended Side Angle pose is both a strength and flexibility posture. It increases your stamina and stimulates the abdominal organs. It stretches the "in seams" and "outer seams" of the body, such as the waistline, groin, and inner thigh.

Extended Side Angle pose strengthens: Quadriceps, hamstrings, core (transverse abdominis, quadratus lumborum), calf, buttocks

Extended Side Angle pose stretches: Hip, inner thigh, core (oblique, quadratus lumborum), upper back (latissimus dorsi), shoulders, biceps

Complementary strength exercises: Walking lunges, single leg press/extension/curl, Stability Oblique lift

Complementary yoga postures: Triangle pose, Side Plank pose, Warrior 2

From Warrior 2 position, inhale and then exhale as you bend from your right lower ribs to place your hand on the big-toe side on the floor (or on a yoga block). Extend your left arm over your left ear. Turn

Modification

Exhale   Inhale   Exhale   Inhale/Exhale Inhale/Exhale Inhale   Exhale

your chin toward your left armpit and gaze toward the left fingertips. Make sure your right knee is parallel to your ankle and that you use your thigh strength. Keep weight evenly on both feet. Keep your torso light and open. It should feel as if you are turning your navel and heart toward the sky. Hold for 5 breath cycles. Inhale and return to Warrior 2. Fully exhale at the top of the posture. Inhale to Attention pose. Exhale in place. Repeat using the left side.

If you can take it further, move into binding by moving your left arm behind your back and right arm under your right thigh. Join hands. Make sure you maintain the extension through your body. Interlace your fingers. Hold for 5 breath cycles.

Exhale. Rewind back to Extended Side Angle pose. Inhale and return to Warrior 2. Exhale to Attention pose. Repeat on the left side.

FOCUS ON FORM

Breath/Focus: It's important to feel openness and lightness in your torso. If you feel crunched in, it will be hard to breathe. Gaze toward your biceps.

Ground: You are grounding through both of your feet and lightly on one hand.

Center: Adjust your pelvis to a neutral position. If you find your buttocks pushing out, draw it into the center.

Expand: Lift your breastbone, relax your shoulders, and draw your shoulder blades down and together.

Lengthen: Feel length through your spine, then lengthen and extend from the outside of your left foot through your whole body to the crown of your head.

BALANCING ON ONE FOOT

Extended Hand to Big Toe Pose

Benefit: Extended Hand to Big Toe pose is both a strength and a flexibility posture. A lot of flexibility is needed to stretch your hamstrings and inner thighs. This pose encourages you to create full body extension, while increasing your ability to balance on one leg. Practicing this pose will improve your posture, strengthen your nervous system, and increase your concentration and sense of self-control. A sense of play, discovery, and honesty will help you master this pose. Take your time and don't fake it.

Extended Hand to Big Toe pose strengthens: On standing leg: foot, ankle, quadriceps, biceps, shoulder (rear), core (transverse abdominis), upper back (trapezius, rhomboid)

Extended Hand to Bitg Toe pose stretches: On extended leg: calf, hamstring, inner thigh

Complementary strength exercises: Single leg squat, single leg press/extension/curl

Complementary yoga postures: Back-Stretching pose, Reclined Hand to Big Toe pose

From Attention pose, gaze at a spot in front of you and draw your right knee to your chest. Interlace your fingers around your right knee and hold them there. Once you are comfortable, place your left hand on your left hip and reach for your right big toe with the first two fin-

Modification   Modification

Exhale   Inhale   Inhale/Exhale Exhale/Inhale Inhale/Exhale Inhale/Exhale   Exhale

gers and thumb of your right hand. Make sure that you maintain the extension of your spine throughout this movement. If you feel stable enough, extend your right leg while holding your toe. Make sure to maintain your posture and take the leg out as far as you can. (If you start rounding your upper back, you've gone too far.)

Hold for 3 to 5 breath cycles. Then open to the right side and look to your left. If looking left throws you off, keep gazing in front of you. Hold for another 3 to 5 breath cycles. Then move your right leg back to center and, depending on your strength and stability, either interlace your fingers and hold your right knee (for support) to extend the leg, or extend the leg without support (but adjust the leg depending on how high you can maintain it). (If you are really in the mood, extend your arms.)

Hold for another 3 to 5 breath cycles, return to Attention pose, and repeat using the left leg.

FOCUS ON FORM

Breath/Focus: Deep breathing is essential in this pose. The more you can relax, the better. Find a spot to gaze into as described, but extend that by trying to focus on your body balancing as a whole.

Ground: It's important to spread your toes so you can get as much support from your foot as possible. Engage your quadriceps muscle.

Center: The hand on the hip should monitor that the pelvis is in neutral. Keep your hips parallel and avoid hiking the right hip up.

Expand: Lifting your breastbone creates room for breath and helps you draw your shoulder blades together, providing support for the upper spine.

Lengthen: You are lengthening first and foremost through your spine. It is important that you adjust your legs in response to how your upper body (spine) is responding to the movements and holding positions throughout the pose. You want to be long and lifted through the spine, not rounded or hunched. The further you move yourself into the posture, the more you need to lift yourself.

Warrior 3

Benefit: Warrior 3 is both a strength and a flexibility pose. This pose promotes full body integration, improves nerve coordination, and increases strength. Practicing Warrior 3 is like playing on a seesaw as a child. A sense of play is helpful in the balancing poses. If you lose your balance, try again; the more you lose your balance, the more it will help you to balance—just keep breathing.

Warrior 3 strengthens: Quadriceps, buttocks, hamstrings, calf, core (transverse abdominis, erector spinae)

Warrior 3 stretches: Hip flexor, entire spine, chest, shoulders

Complementary strength exercises: Single squat, single leg press/extension/curl, stability plank

Complementary yoga postures: Fierce pose, Locust pose, Extended Hand to Big Toe pose

From Attention pose place your hands on your hips and extend your left leg behind you while keeping the foot flexed. Keep your focus toward the floor. Shift your weight onto your right leg and foot. Start hinging forward from your hips until your leg and spine are horizontal to the floor. You might not be able to move this far without falling over, but move as far as you can while still holding your balance. Maintain the position you can and move on from there. When you can move further, extend your arms above your head. Hold for 3 to 5 breath cycles. Inhale as you rewind the pose until your spine is vertical to the floor and exhale. Return to Attention pose.

Exhale/Inhale Exhale/Inhale Exhale/Inhale Exhale/Inhale Inhale Exhale

FOCUS ON FORM

Breath/Focus: Keep looking toward the floor with a long neck and the breath flowing the whole time.

Ground: You are grounding from your right foot. Keep your toes spread and your foot evenly placed. The right quad is actively contracted.

Center: Make sure that your pelvis remains in a neutral position and that your hips stay squared off. Keep your core muscles active so they can support you.

Expand: Try to lift your breastbone to keep your torso open and expansive and feel the length of your spine. Draw the shoulder blades down and together to keep space between your ears and your shoulders.

Lengthen: First and foremost, lengthen through your spine, and then work the extension from your left heel through your spine to the crown of your head.

ARM BALANCES

Hand Stand

Benefit: Hand stand is primarily a strength posture, with some shoulder flexibility involved. We can also call this posture Downward-Facing Attention pose. It's the same movement, except now you're grounding through your arms instead of your feet. The biggest obstacle when doing this pose is the fear of being turned upside-down and a lack of trust in your arms. With practice, you will overcome your fear by taking your time and releasing the pressure. Don't struggle; find a way and trust yourself. With consistent practice, this will happen!

Hand stand strengthens: Triceps, wrists, hands, upper back muscles (trapezius, rhomboids, latissimus dorsi), shoulders, core (transverse abdominis, erector spinae), entire spine

Hand stand stretches: Chest, shoulders

Complementary strength exercises: Gravitron: wide pull-up, biceps pull-up, triceps dips

Complementary yoga postures: Downward-Facing Dog pose

Position yourself close to a wall in a Downward-Facing Dog position, keep your hands shoulder-width apart. Look forward toward the wall. Walk your feet halfway to your hands. Your hips will lift into the air. Inhale as you bend your knees slightly and push off legs with the ball of your right foot. Exhale at the top. Once you are up, keep breathing deep but smooth breaths. Get used to balancing on the hands and arms and eventually work one leg at a time away from the wall until both are away from the wall. Gaze at a spot between your hands. Work up to staying in this position for 5 to 15 breath cycles. Slowly lower one leg at a time, controlling this motion, to the floor. Don't lower with a clunk. Return to the starting position. Rest in Child's pose for about 5 breath cycles to regain your equilibrium.

FOCUS ON FORM

Breath/Focus: Breathe as deeply as possible. Stay aware of how your body responds to the work—and how your mind responds to being turned upside-down.

Ground: You are grounding through the palms of your hands. It's important to spread your fingers and press your palms against the floor to get a feeling of lifting yourself out of your wrists.

Center: You want to avoid creating what's called a banana—meaning an excessive sway in your back. So work your pelvis into a neutral position (think Attention pose on your hands) by drawing your ribs in and keeping your core muscles active.

Modification

Exhale   Inhale/Exhale Inhale/Exhale Inhale/Exhale Exhale/Inhale Exhale/Inhale

Expand: You need to keep your shoulders engaged, but relaxed. Draw them away from your ears, keep the shoulder blades down and into the back, and lift the breastbone.

Lengthen: How you position your pelvis is crucial to your ability to lengthen yourself. Try to flex your feet so you can get a better sense of being grounded through your hands. Once you feel the length through your spine you'll be able to better engage your core muscles and this will help you gain improved control.

FORWARD BENDING POSTURE

Marichyasana A

Benefit: Marichyasana A is both a strength and a flexibility posture, with an emphasis on flexibility in the shoulders, spine, hips, and hamstrings. This posture will help you be patient and create openings.

Marichyasana A strengthens: Core (transverse abdominis), upper back muscles (rhomboids, trapezius); extended leg: quadriceps, shin, ankle

Marichyasana A stretches: Entire spine, lower/middle/upper back, chest, shoulders (anterior, rotator cuffs), biceps, wrists; extended leg: hamstring; bent leg: hip

Complementary strength exercises: Single leg press/extension, Gravitron pull-up, seated row

Complementary yoga postures: Back-Stretching pose, Locust pose, Bow pose

Modification

Exhale   Inhale   Inhale/Exhale   Inhale/Exhale   Exhale

From Stick pose, draw your right knee toward your chest with your right foot grounded on the floor and your heel in front of your right sitting bone. Keep your left arm at your left side for support. Inhale as you extend your right arm forward and try to get your right shoulder in front of your right shin. Exhale as you internally rotate your right shoulder so that you can bend the elbow to bind behind your back with your left hand. Once you're bound, inhale as you lengthen your spine and then exhale as you hinge forward over your left leg. Keep the left foot flexed and the left quadriceps contracted.

If you find it challenging, practice with a towel or yoga rope. Work toward holding your left foot with both hands. Once you have achieved this, you can work your arm behind your back to bind. Stay in the pose for 5 to 10 breath cycles.

Inhale as you look up and exhale as you move into Stick pose. Repeat, using the left side.

FOCUS ON FORM

Breath/Focus: Keep your gaze toward your left big toe. Breathe and exhale fully. This is not an easy position to be in, but it gets easier if you create space with your breath.

Ground: You are grounding through your pelvis. It's not easy to ground in this position with one leg bent and one leg extended. This is why it is doubly important to get lift in your torso. Both sitting bones are grounded.

Center: Allow your pelvis to tilt forward slightly (as in Stick pose) so your tailbone moves back. This way you can sit at the tips of your sitting bones and create more expansion in your rib cage. As always, core muscles support you.

Expand: Relax your shoulders, draw your shoulder blades down and together, and lift your breastbone. This will help you breathe and create more length in your spine.

Lengthen: You are lengthening through your spine. Maintain the extension as time, gravity, and your breath help you bend farther forward.

Pigeon Quad Stretch

Benefits: Pigeon quad stretch is primarily a flexibility posture and is part of a backward-bending posture called Full Pigeon pose. In this case, we use it to stretch the muscles in your front body, in particular the quadriceps and hip flexors. This posture will leave you refreshed and open to face the challenges that come your way. Make yourself comfortable. It *is* possible to breathe in this position. If this posture doesn't agree withh your knees, do the Half Frog pose instead.

Pigeon quad stretch strengthens: Buttocks, hamstrings, upper back muscles (trapezius, rhomboids), shoulders (rear), core (transverse abdominis, erector spinae)

Pigeon quad stretch stretches: Quadriceps, hip flexors, shin, ankle, buttocks, entire spine, shoulders (anterior), biceps, core (rectus abdominis)

Complementary strength exercises: Single hamstring curl, single leg squat

Complementary yoga postures: Frog pose, Bow pose

From Downward-Facing Dog pose slide your right leg into a basic Pigeon pose. Bend your left leg and hold your left ankle with your left hand, or with both hands. Keep your gaze forward toward the sky. Stay in the pose for 5 to 10 breath cycles. If you feel stable and ready for a more intense stretch, slowly exhale as you bend forward to lower your

Modification

Exhale   Inhale/Exhale Inhale/Exhale Inhale/Exhale Inhale/Exhale   Exhale   Inhale/Exhale

chest and forehead to the floor with either a single grip or with a double grip. Inhale to lift back up. Exhale to release out of the pose and push back to Downward-Facing Dog pose. Repeat using the left leg. When you've completed both sides, rest in Child's pose for 3 to 5 breath cycles.

FOCUS ON FORM

Breath/Focus: The bigger your breath is, the easier it will be to do this. Be aware of how your body responds to the position, especially your lower back area.

Ground: You are grounded through your pelvis, front leg, and back thigh. It's more important that your hips be squared off than that they are grounded to the floor. Neither your pelvis nor shoulders should rotate. This rotation can happen easily if the quadriceps and hip flexors are tight.

Center: Keep your tailbone drawn under to engage the core muscles and support your lower back.

Expand: Relax your shoulders, draw your shoulder blades down and together and lift your breastbone. The more grounded and centered you are, the more you can expand through your heart.

Lengthen: Feel the length through your spine, from your tailbone to the crown of your head. It takes time to feel comfortable in this position. Keep working with it and you'll begin to feel the length and extension of your spine.

Wheel Pose

Benefit: Wheel pose involves both strength and shoulder/spine flexibility. If you are strong, it's about flexibility. If you are flexible, it is more a matter of strength. There is full body integration in trying to connect the limbs together with the torso. If you are feeling the blues, practice a few wheels; this will open you up to the world and give you new perspective, and you'll be ready to go.

When performing this asana it is very important to find your own place to start. We're going to do it in stages since this is a challenging

pose. We start with $^1/_2$ wheel (also called Bridge pose), then move to what I call $^3/_4$ wheel, and last, full wheel.

Wheel pose strengthens: Upper back muscles (trapezius, rhomboid, serratus anterior), triceps, rear shoulder, forearms, wrists, fingers, hamstrings, buttocks, calves

Wheel pose stretches: Entire spine, quadriceps, hip flexors, core abdomen, chest, front shoulders, spine

Complementary strength exercises: Triceps dips, leg press

Complementary flexibility exercises: Upward-Facing Dog pose, Bow pose, Cow's Face pose

From Stick Pose lie down on your back, arms alongside your body. Bend both legs and place feet hip-width apart and parallel.

$^1/_2$ *wheel:* Inhale. Lift your pelvis off the floor. Lift your breastbone and draw your shoulder blades toward each other to interlace your fingers. Hold for 5 breath cycles. Focus toward the ceiling.

$^3/_4$ *wheel:* From $^1/_2$ wheel position, extend your arms to the ceiling, bend your elbows, and place your hands behind your shoulders next to your ears. Inhale as you press your palms against the floor to lift yourself to the crown of your head; exhale when you're there. Focus at a spot in front of you. Hold for 5 breath cycles.

Full wheel: From $^3/_4$ wheel, inhale as you press your palms against the floor to straighten your arms. Exhale at the top. Focus on a spot in front of you. Hold for 5 breath cycles; if you've gone too far, rewind back to $^3/_4$ or $^1/_2$ wheel.

Modification   Modification

Exhale   Inhale   Exhale   Inhale/Exhale   Inhale/Exhale   Exhale   Exhale/Inhale

Exhale while you draw your chin to your chest and roll down to the floor vertebra by vertebra, starting at the upper back, then middle back, and last, lower back, returning to starting position. Repeat this two to three times. After that, counter pose with back stretching pose for 5 to 10 breath cycles.

FOCUS ON FORM

Breath/Focus: Make sure you don't hold your breath when you practice these. Focus on lifting with the inhalation. Be mindful of how your body reacts to this position and always adjust either further into it or further out of it.

Ground: You are grounding through your hands and feet. It's important you "put your mind into your feet and hands." They easily move all over the place when bending backward like this. Feet should be parallel or slightly pigeon-toed. If you feel pain in your wrists, spread your fingers and press your palms against the floor. During the rest, make a fist with your hands and do wrist circles to release the tension. They'll get stronger over time. You can also use the Gripitz yoga prop as mentioned under arm balancing poses. (See the resource guide.)

Center: As you lift into the position, tuck the tailbone under slightly to engage your core muscles for lower back support and stability.

Expand: Keep your breastbone lifted, roll your shoulders back, and draw your shoulder blades together. Straighten your legs so that it feels as if you are stretching your heart to the back wall.

Lengthen: You are decompressing your spine in this position. Work gracefully and with respect. Maintain full extension through the spine, regardless of what position you're in.

RELAXATION

I bet the relaxation part is going better now, and your mind is letting go a little bit more. Continue from Level 2 and position yourself into your Savasana position.

In Level 3 you perform a counting exercise I call "counting to stillness." Choose a number, say the number 15, and count your breath cycles up to the number 15. When you have mastered that number, increase it by 5. This is what you do: Mentally repeat to yourself,

I am breathing in 1, I am breathing out 1.

I am breathing in 2. I am breathing out 2.

I am breathing in 3. I am breathing out 3.

Work yourself up to the number 15. If you get distracted on the fifth breath, think the thought through, try to let it go, and start from the beginning and see how far you get this time.

This practice is an attempt to further still your mind. Being able to stay focused on one thing for a longer period of time will help you develop increased concentration and attention span. In return you receive energy back tenfold.

Level 3 Strength Training

LOWER BODY

BODY WEIGHT

Single Leg Squat

Benefit: The single leg squat is lovely. It will give strength, tone, and balance to your lower body. Everything you've worked on thus far is put to the test and integrated into this one. Although this exercise uses only body weight, it's quite challenging and, don't worry, you'll feel the burn.

Muscles being strengthened: Hip flexors, quadriceps, buttocks, hamstrings, ankle, shin

Assisting: Core muscles (transverse abdominis, erector spinae)

Complementary strength poses: Standing balancing postures on one leg: Eagle pose, Extended Hand to Big Toe pose

Complementary flexibility poses: Seated postures, and particularly Pigeon quad stretch, seated/standing forward bend

From the ready position, lift your right leg off the floor and keep your foot at ankle height, close to the inside of your left foot. Keep your focus on the floor in front of you. Start with placing both hands on your hips. As you progress, free your right hand to touch your left foot.

Bend the left leg at your hip and knee (as you did in a regular squat) and lean into your left heel. Draw the tailbone backward to tilt the pelvis forward, but keep the core muscles active to avoid arching

Modification

Modification

Exhale   Inhale/Exhale   Inhale   Inhale   Inhale   Exhale

the lower spine. Bend and lower so much that you (over time) can touch your left foot with your right fingers.

Inhale as you lower; exhale as you lift. Complete 10 to 15 repetitions. Return to ready position and repeat on the left side.

FOCUS ON FORM

Breath/Focus: Make sure you keep your focus on the floor in front of you throughout the exercise. Do not squat so low that it inhibits your breathing. Always inhale as you lower, exhale as you lift.

Ground: You are balancing on one foot here, so you are grounding through the foot and leg on which you are standing. Press your foot against the floor (as if you're doing a leg press) to help center your pelvis, allowing you to expand through your heart.

Center: It's important when you're balancing on one leg that you don't throw your pelvis forward. Start with placing your hands on your hips to make sure your hips are balanced and squared off. Your strength and balance will determine how far you can lower yourself. Keep your core muscles active and remain aware of how your pelvis is responding to the single leg squat.

Expand: Keep your breastbone lifted and your shoulders relaxed. It's important to keep your chest lifted; you should not be hinging forward from your hips. The legs are in charge—the torso is "just following."

Lengthen: You are lengthening through your spine. If you center and expand, this will take care of itself.

MACHINE

Single Leg Press

Benefit: The single leg press is designed to strengthen each leg individually while building power, tone, and stability in your lower body muscles.

There are different types of leg press machines. Try to alternate between the type in which you push the weight away from you and the kind in which you have to push your body away. If you don't have access to a leg press you can do squats and lunges instead.

Muscles being strengthened and stretched: Buttocks, quadriceps, hamstrings, calves

Assisting: Belly (transverse abdominis)

Complementary strength poses: Standing postures, balancing on one leg

Complementary flexibility poses: Reclined Extended Hand to Big Toe pose, Half Frog pose

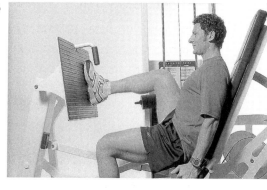

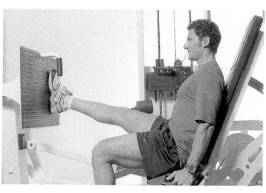

Choose your weight and adjust the back pad for comfort and to allow a full range of motion. Lean back and rest your back and head on the back pad. Position one leg on the board and leave the other leg resting. Hold onto the handles. Exhale as you extend your leg by pressing your foot against the plate (more from your heel than your forefoot). Inhale as you return to starting position by bending your leg, drawing your knees toward your chest. Do 12 to 15 repetitions and repeat on the other leg.

FOCUS ON FORM

Breath/Focus: Keep your gaze in front of you. Your breath should be full and deep to match the intense work of the leg press. Exhale as you extend the leg; inhale as you bend the leg.

Ground: You are grounded through your pelvis. Your upper body is stationary, which gives you a great advantage in putting extra force on

Inhale   Exhale

your leg muscles. Make sure you contract your quadriceps as you extend your leg, and press from your heel. Avoid hyperextending your knees as you extend your leg.

Center: Position the pelvis so your lower back is protected. Engage the press from the core and keep these muscles active. Avoid sinking into the hip.

Expand: Keep your breastbone lifted, your shoulders relaxed, and your shoulder blades drawn together. Rest your head against the back pad and make sure that you are not straining your neck muscles.

Lengthen: You are lengthening through your spine. Make sure, even if your spine is supported by the back pad, that the weight you have chosen doesn't cause too much pressure on the lower spine.

Single Leg Curl

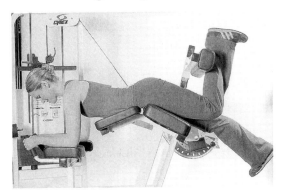

Benefit: The single leg curl is designed to strengthen each leg individually while building strength and tone in the back of your thigh (your hamstring muscle).

Muscle being strengthened: Hamstring

Assisting: Core muscles (transverse abdominis, erector spinae), buttocks, biceps, upper back muscles (trapezius, rhomboids)

Complementary strength poses: Backward-bending postures such as Locust pose, Bow pose

Complementary flexibility poses: Downward-Facing Dog pose, Back-Stretching pose

Inhale   Exhale

Lie on your belly and adjust your pelvis to a neutral position. Focus on a spot on the floor. Hold onto the handlebars. Keep your breastbone lifted and engage your shoulder blades. Keep your feet flexed. As you bend your right leg, let the left leg rest. Exhale to bend your leg, moving your heel toward the buttocks. Inhale as you extend (avoid hyperextending your knee). Do 12 to 15 repetitions. Repeat using the left leg.

FOCUS ON FORM

Breath/Focus: Exhale as you curl; inhale as you extend. Gaze at a spot on the floor while being mindful of how your lower back responds to the leg curl.

Ground: You are grounding through your pelvis.

Center: Do not let your hip bones lift off the bench or collapse into one hip. Keep your tailbone drawn under and use your core muscles to maintain a neutral pelvis. Avoid "crunching" the lower back muscles. Keeping your pelvis motionless will isolate the hamstring.

Expand: Keep your breastbone lifted, shoulders relaxed, and shoulder blades together. This will help you create space in your rib cage to breathe fully.

Lengthen: Maintain length in your spine, from your tailbone to the crown of your head. Keep your head lifted.

Single Leg Extension

Benefit: The single leg extension is designed to strengthen each leg individually while building strength and tone in the front of your thigh (the quadriceps muscle).

Muscles being strengthened: Quadriceps

Assisting: Core muscles (transverse abdominis), upper back muscles (trapezius, rhomboids), biceps

Complementary strength poses: The leg extension will help you isolate your quadriceps for poses such as one leg balancing poses,

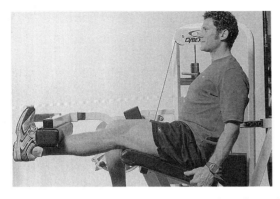

standing side lateral bends, and twists.

Complementary flexibility poses: Upward-Facing Dog pose, Half Frog pose, Bow pose

Position the back rest and leg rest to fit your body. Place one foot on the leg rest and let the other foot rest on the side. Keep feet flexed, hold the handle bar, and keep your rib cage lifted. Focus on a spot in front of you. Exhale as you contract your quadriceps to extend your leg (avoid hyperextending the knees) and inhale as you bend your leg (avoid bending so much that the weights touch). Do 12 to 15 repetitions and repeat using the other leg.

FOCUS ON FORM

Breath/Focus: Exhale as you extend the leg, inhale as you bend the leg. Keep your focus on a spot in front of you while being aware of working your quadriceps.

Ground: You are grounding through your pelvis.

Center: Pelvis is tilted slightly forward to center on your sitting bones. Draw your power from your core muscles.

Expand: Keep the breastbone lifted, shoulders relaxed, and shoulder blades drawn down, holding onto the handlebar on the machine and engaging the biceps. Lift your rib cage out of your hips to make room for deep breaths and good isolation of the quadriceps.

Lengthen: Keep your spine vertical and lengthened. Don't work with more weight than will allow you to keep your spine lengthened without hunching forward.

Inhale   Exhale

Unilateral Stability Pull-In

Benefit: The unilateral stability pull-in is designed to challenge each side of the body independently while developing balanced strength and stability.

Muscles being strengthened (the same muscles need stretching): Core muscles (transverse abdominis, oblique, erector spinae), upper back muscles (trapezius, latissimus dorsi, rhomboids, serratus anterior), triceps, wrists, quadriceps, buttocks

Complementary strength poses: Arm balancing postures such as Crow pose, Side Plank pose

Complementary flexibility poses: Upward-Facing Dog pose, Downward-Facing Dog pose

Position yourself in Stability Plank pose from Level 2. Inhale to lift your right leg off the ball, then exhale as you pull your left knee in toward your chest. Inhale to extend the left leg, exhale to lower the right leg back to the ball. Repeat using the left leg. Do 5 to 10 repetitions on each leg, or as many as you can manage without collapsing.

FOCUS ON FORM

Breath/Focus: Keep your gaze on a spot on the floor. Your breath should be smooth and even. Inhale as you lift the leg, exhale as you pull in, inhale as you extend, exhale as you release and lower your leg back to the ball.

Ground: You are mostly grounding through your hand and arms.

Center: Keep the pelvis in a neutral position with core muscles engaged to avoid allowing the pelvis to sink and create an arch in the lower back.

Inhale/Exhale   Inhale   Exhale   Inhale   Exhale

Expand: Keep your torso motionless as your leg bends and extends. Nothing but the leg should be moving. Keep your breastbone lifted so that you can roll your shoulders back. Draw your shoulder blades into your back for upper back support.

Lengthen: Maintain extension in your spine (avoid dropping your head) to allow for full body integration.

Stability Back Extension

Benefit: The stability back extension is designed to strengthen your back body muscles.

Muscles being strengthened: Core muscles (transverse abdominis, erector spinae), buttocks, hamstrings, upper back muscles (trapezius, rhomboids, latissimus dorsi)

Complementary strength pose: Locust pose

Complementary flexibility pose: Child's pose

Position your body over the ball, face down, legs extended and supported against the wall. Place your arms behind your head and point your elbows outward. Exhale as you fold over the ball; inhale as you roll up vertebra by vertebra to a fully extended position while contracting your buttocks and lower back muscles. Repeat 10 to 15 times.

FOCUS ON FORM

Breath/Focus: Exhale as you lower; inhale as you lift. Keep your focus on a spot in front of you.

Ground: You are grounding through your pelvis and feet. It might be challenging at first to feel grounded on the ball, but as you practice, you will become more stable.

Inhale   Exhale

Center: Draw your tailbone under and engage your lower abdominal muscles. As you lift, make sure you engage your buttock muscles to avoid lifting too high (not good for your lower back).

Expand: You should feel as though you are lifting your rib cage out of your hips. Keep the breastbone lifted and shoulders rolled back to draw the shoulder blades into your back for upper back support.

Lengthen: You are lengthening through your spine and extending from your feet to the crown of your head.

CHEST

Bench Press

Benefit: The bench press is designed to increase your muscular strength and has an element of balance involved as well. If you don't have a barbell, use free weights instead. This exercise gives you a lot of power and stability for the arm balancing postures. Chaturanga will become a "piece of cake." You will gain a lot of confidence.

Muscles being strengthened: Chest

Muscles assisting: Triceps, shoulders (anterior, rotator cuff, teres major), back muscles (latissimus dorsi, serratus anterior, rhomboids)

Inhale   Exhale

Complementary strength poses: Crow pose, hand stand

Complementary flexibility poses: Bow pose, Wheel pose

Place the amount of weight that you can handle on the bar. Make sure you have secured the plates with the safety clips! And it's always a good idea to have a spotter. People will be more than happy to give you a spot; just ask.

Lie down on the bench with your feet on the bench. Adjust your pelvis into a neutral position. Make sure your spine is long and supported. Take hold of the bar. Find the mark on the bar where your arms are at a 90-degree angle. Place the bar in line with your breastbone. Inhale as you lower the bar to almost touch your chest. Feel your chest expanding. Exhale as you contract the chest muscles and extend the arms. Do 12 to 15 repetitions. If you can't do that many reps, try it with less weight.

FOCUS ON FORM

Breath/Focus: Inhale as you lower; exhale as you lift. You need very deep expansive breaths for this one! Focus at a spot on the ceiling while you "see" your arms moving and feel your chest and arms working.

Ground: You are grounding through your back body and feet.

Center: Maintain a neutral spine and make sure your core muscles support you.

Expand: With support from your core you can better keep your breastbone lifted. Roll the shoulders back to draw the shoulder blades together for upper back support. This will also help you isolate the chest muscles.

Lengthen: You are lengthening through your spine, from your tailbone to the crown of your head.

GRAVITRON EXERCISES

I am forever grateful for the invention of the Gravitron. The Gravitron is a machine that will help you to do pull-ups and dips by assisting you in lifting only a percentage of your body weight. Set the machine to your body weight minus 20 to 40 pounds. The more weight you use, the easier it is. How many people can do an unsupported pull-up? Not many; but the gravitron will give you all the assistance you need until you can do one on your own! It's of great help in gaining strength in your upper back and arm muscles.

If you are one of those fortunate people who can do unassisted pull-ups, continue with these and follow the "focus on form" suggestions.

Assisted Wide Pull-Ups

Benefit: The assisted wide pull-up is designed to strengthen your upper back muscles and give you that beautiful V-shaped back. This is often called a chin-up and is usually done with a narrow grip. A wider grip works the muscles of the back a bit better, however. You can always alternate wide and narrow grips.

Muscles strengthened: Upper back muscles (trapezius, rhomboids, latissimus dorsi), shoulders (posterior, teres major, levator scapulae)

Assisting: Biceps, core muscles

Complementary strength poses: Hand stand, shoulder stand

Complementary flexibility poses: Extended side angle, Marichyasana A

Inhale   Exhale

Find your perfect weight. Some Gravitrons have you place your knees on a pad; others have you place your feet on a bar. Grip the handle-bars. Exhale as you pull yourself up; inhale as you slowly lower yourself back down. Do 12 to 15 repetitions.

FOCUS ON FORM

Breath/Focus: Exhale as you lift; inhale as you lower. Your breath should be deep and expansive.

Ground: You are grounding through your legs.

Center: Keep your core muscles active to stabilize your pelvis. This will help you create lightness in your body and keep the lower back from arching.

Expand: Keep your breastbone lifted; focus on the back muscles and not the biceps, shoulders, or neck to lift you. Avoid leading with your chin.

Lengthen: You are lengthening through your spine. Avoid tensing your neck.

SHOULDERS

Single shoulder press on one leg

Benefit: The single shoulder press on one leg is designed to shape and strengthen the individual shoulder and leg.

Muscles being strengthened: Middle shoulder, upper back (upper trapezius, serratus anterior), triceps

Complementary strength poses: Side Plank pose

Complementary flexibility poses: Eagle pose

From a ready position, lift your right leg off the floor and keep this foot at ankle height. Hold your right hand on your right hip and, with a dumbbell in your left hand, lift your left arm from your elbow to shoulder level. Exhale as you push the dumbbell above your head (without hyperextending your elbow). Inhale as you return to shoulder level. Do 12 to 15 repetitions.

FOCUS ON FORM

Breath/Focus: Focus on a spot in front of you while you exhale as you extend the arm. Inhale as you bend.

Ground: You are grounding through your left foot. Keep foot parallel and spread your toes.

Center: Keep your pelvis in a neutral position in order to firmly center and support the core muscles. This makes sure that you don't favor one side.

Expand: Lift your breastbone and roll your shoulders back, drawing the shoulder blades toward each other to avoid moving the shoulders up to the ears as you extend the arm.

Lengthen: You are lengthening through your spine.

Inhale   Exhale

Assisted Biceps Pull-Up

Benefit: Assisted biceps pull-up is designed to develop strength and tone in the front of your upper arm (your biceps muscle). It will give you "arms of steel."

Muscles being strengthened: Biceps

Complementary strength poses: Shoulder stand, Downward-Facing Dog pose

Complementary flexibility poses: Extended Side Angle pose (binding), Cow's Face pose

Find your perfect weight. Some Gravitrons have you place your knees on a pad; others have you place your feet on a bar. Grip the upper middle handlebars. Exhale as you pull yourself up. Inhale as you slowly lower yourself back down. Do 12 to 15 repetitions.

FOCUS ON FORM

Breath/Focus: Exhale as you lift; inhale as you lower. Your breath should be very deep and expansive.

Ground: You are grounding through your legs.

Center: Keep your core muscles active in order to stabilize your pelvis. This helps you create lightness in your body and keep the lower back from arching.

Expand: Keep your breastbone lifted, and focus on the biceps muscles and core muscles lifting you. Avoid leading with your chin.

Lengthen: You are lengthening through your spine. Avoid tensing your neck.

Inhale   Exhale

Assisted Triceps Dip

Benefit: The assisted triceps dip is designed to strengthen and tone the muscle on the back of your upper arm (your triceps muscle). This is often a problem area for women. No more, if you add this one to your workout.

Muscles being strengthened: Triceps

Complementary strength poses: Hand stand, Plank pose, Crow pose

Complementary flexibility poses: Cow's Face pose

Find your perfect weight. Some Gravitrons have you place your knees on a pad; others have you place you feet on a bar. Grip the handlebars. Exhale as you pull yourself up. Inhale as you slowly lower yourself back down. Do 12 to 15 repetitions.

FOCUS ON FORM

Breath/Focus: Inhale as you lower, exhale as you lift. Your breath should be very deep and expansive.

Ground: You are grounding through your legs.

Center: Keep your core muscles active in order to stabilize your pelvis. This helps you create lightness in your body and keep the lower back from arching.

Expand: Keep your breastbone lifted, and focus on the back muscles and not the biceps, shoulders, or neck to lift you. Avoid leading with your chin. Do not lower your shoulder farther than elbow height.

Lengthen: You are lengthening through your spine. Avoid tensing your neck.

Inhale   Exhale

Level 3 Endurance

AEROBIC ENDURANCE ACTIVITIES

EXERCISE SELECTION: STAIRMASTER

The stairmaster is exactly what it implies, like walking the stairs. I used to live in a fifth-floor walkup and dreaded the stairs but amused myself by using the stairmaster several times a week. Try to figure that one out!

The stairmaster gives you extra leg work, with lower impact than running. It can be a nice change for the muscles. The movement is confined to the machine.

Supportive Conditioning Exercises

Muscles often overtaxed that need flexibility: feet, ankles, hip flexors, shoulders, neck, lower back, calves, hamstrings, quadriceps

Muscles often underutilized that need strength: Upper back muscles, lower back, core, arms, shoulders

Stairmaster Posture/Technique

The posture for the stairmaster is much the same as for running and the elliptical machine. Compared to the elliptical there is slightly more impact on the lower body muscles.

The stairmaster is similar to holding the standing balancing poses for several breaths. You are stationary but at the same time you are "moving" because you are adapting your physical body to the activity. You are constantly being tested to fit your posture to the machine, matching both of your "tools."

You are grounding through your feet, centering through your pelvis and core, expanding through your rib cage, and lengthening through your spine.

Be sure to use your own support system—your skeleton. Avoid hunching and relying on the rails to support you. Don't "crank up the volume" if you can't support it and end up hunching. Slow down the pace and don't hold onto the handlebars; you'll have to use your core strength and balance more.

A hunched posture makes the upper back muscles too flexible and the chest muscles too tight, makes it harder to breathe and get the energy moving throughout your body. It also causes a tight shoulder and neck and has a negative impact on your lower back and hamstrings.

The stronger your upper body is, the more your legs can work. A combination of strength and flexibility in your legs will help your upper body relax. A strong core will bridge your upper body and your lower body so that they will work together in unison.

Lower Body

It is important to place your feet parallel on the platforms with your toes spread. This can be a challenge on the stairmaster if you have big feet; the platforms are often too small and half the foot is off the platform. Place your foot in the middle of the platform so you can press down through your heel.

Keep your feet parallel and press back through the heel, using the back thigh muscles; specifically, the gluteus and hamstrings. Don't hyperextend the knee. Contract your quad muscles as you press down. Actively lift your legs and alternate the push and pull action, working both legs evenly.

Core

As in running, your pelvis should be in a neutral position with room to move. Allow the core muscles to provide stability and support. Avoid any arching of your lower back.

Upper Body

Keep your shoulders relaxed, your shoulder blades drawn down and slightly together, and your breastbone lifted. Try not to hold the rails. If you must, hold them lightly. This will force you to use your core and balance. Keep your arms bent but relaxed at your sides. Your intensity should be such that you need not hold the rails.

The Warm-Up

Incorporating the Sun Salutations into your warm-up is very helpful because they give your upper body strength and stretch your feet, ankles, legs, hip flexors, shoulders, chest, and spine. The Sun Salutations also help to prevent shin splints and are very user friendly for your feet. Rolling over the toes from Chaturanga to Upward-Facing Dog and Downward-Facing Dog will increase circulation and also balance the calf and shin muscles.

The Warm-Down

It's important to do both forward-bending and backward-bending poses to balance and strengthen the muscles of the front and back body. Twists are important, too, for hip and spinal flexibility. These poses also add core strength.

Focus

Try not to distract yourself by reading a magazine or looking at TV. Find a spot in front of you where you can focus and pay attention to your alignment during the activity. Count your breaths and steps and visualize yourself stepping to the top of the Empire State Building.

Flow and Energy

Try to coordinate your breathing with your movement. Deep diaphragmatic breathing is recommended. Keep the shoulders relaxed and length in your spine, and work at a tempo you can physically support. This will make it easier to breathe deep and increase your energy expenditure. Hanging over the rails is a sign that the intensity is too high. Slow down and stand erect. You'll burn more calories, you will look better, and you will feel amazing! Your movement should feel connected and light.

Safety, Caution, and Rest

Don't go faster than what your body can handle. Get used to the machine before you "crank up the volume."

4-Week Stairmaster Program

WEEK	PROGRAM	MINUTES	INTENSITY
1	Warm-up phase	3–5	50 %
	Target heart rate phase: fat burner program	25–30	60 %
	Warm-down phase	3–5	Resting heart rate + 10 points
2	Warm-up phase	3–5	40–50 %
	Target heart rate phase: steady hill program	25	60–70 %
	Warm-down phase	3–5	Resting heart rate + 10 points
3	Warm-up phase	3–5	40–50 %
	Target heart rate phase: interval program	20–25	60–70 %
	Warm-down phase	3–5	Resting heart rate + 10 points
4	Warm-up phase	3–5	40–50 %
	Target heart rate phase: manual program—have fun making up your own program	25	60 %
	Warm-down phase	3–5	Resting heart rate + 10 points

Should you be walking or running? That depends on what you've chosen to do, and what you *can* do. In the beginning of the program I give you an option to choose what you want to do according to what works for you.

4-week Power Walking Program

WEEK	PROGRAM	MINUTES	INTENSITY
1	Warm-up phase	3–5	40–50 %
	Target heart rate phase: flat	30	60–70 %
	Warm-down phase	3–5	Resting heart rate + 10 points
2	Warm-up phase	3–5	40–50 %
	Target heart rate phase: interval flat/hilly	25	60–70 %
	Warm-down phase	3–5	Resting heart rate + 10 points
3	Warm-up phase	3–5	40–50 %
	Target heart rate phase: flat/very hilly/flat	30	55–65 %
	Warm-down phase	3–5	Resting heart rate + 10 points
4	Warm-up phase	3–5	40–50 %
	Target heart rate phase: flat/hilly/very hilly/flat	30–35	60–70 %
	Warm-down phase	3–5	Resting heart rate + 10 points

4-week Running Program

WEEK	PROGRAM	MINUTES	INTENSITY
1	Warm-up phase	3–5	50 %
	Target heart rate phase: flat	30–35	70–80 %
	Warm-down phase	3–5	Resting heart rate + 10 points
2	Warm-up phase	3–5	40–50 %
	Target heart rate phase: flat/hilly/flat	30	65–75 %
	Warm-down phase	3–5	Resting heart rate + 10 points
3	Warm-up phase	3–5	40–50 %
	Target heart rate phase: flat	30–35	60–70 %
	Warm-down phase	3–5	Resting heart rate + 10 points
4	Warm-up phase	3–5	40–50 %
	Target heart rate phase: flat/hilly/flat	30	65–75 %
	Warm-down phase	3–5	Resting heart rate + 10 points

4-week Biking Program

WEEK	PROGRAM	MINUTES	INTENSITY
1	Warm-up phase	3–5	40–50 %
	Target heart rate phase: flat	30	70–80 %
	Warm-down phase	3–5	Resting heart rate + 10 points
2	Warm-up phase	3–5	40–50 %
	Target heart rate phase: interval flat/hilly	25	60–70 %
	Warm-down phase	3–5	Resting heart rate + 10 points
3	Warm-up phase	3–5	40–50 %
	Target heart rate phase: flat	30	70 %
	Warm-down phase	3–5	Resting heart rate + 10 points
4	Warm-up phase	3–5	40–50 %
	Target heart rate phase: flat/hilly/very hilly/flat	30–35	70 %
	Warm-down phase	3–5	Resting heart rate + 10 points

CHAPTER 6

Your Best Body Ever and Beyond

Congratulations! You made it! You have successfully completed Levels 1, 2 and 3 and are on your way to creating *your* best body ever.

What Your Body Knows

By working through the different levels of this book you now know your body better than ever. The three elements of physical fitness have brought together and fine-tuned your awareness and overall fitness. The result is (deservedly) *your* best body ever—the best version of your evolving self.

You have stretched your edge with yoga postures, worked to failure with strength-training exercises, and tried to avoid "hitting the wall" with aerobic exercises.

You are now at a point where you should reflect, take a look at your body, and prepare to continue the journey, taking *your* best body ever to new and better heights. It doesn't stop here! Completing Level 3 doesn't mean it's over; this is just the beginning. But what happens now? How can you continue to use the Goa System and move beyond Level 3?

Throughout the levels, I have encouraged you to follow the given structure, but at the same time adjust the program according to your time, needs, and lifestyle. I hope you have. By now you know how long it takes to do your workout and you have become very familiar with how each of the elements affects your body. Now is the time to adjust—to decrease, increase, or keep the same the intensity, frequency, and duration of each of the elements of physical fitness: flexibility, strength, and endurance. Moving beyond Level 3 is about customizing your workout program.

Your Best Can Get Even Better

You have learned different strength-training exercises for all of your major body parts, various yoga postures from all of the common yoga categories, and different aerobic exercises. How will you know when to decrease or increase the intensity, frequency, and duration of each element? Here are some body specifics to guide you.

Yoga Flexibility

▲ You never get to a point where you will outgrow the yoga poses. You can always move further into them. If you haven't been doing all of the poses presented, you might now feel ready to add them. Perhaps you will find that you are now more patient with these poses. Take on the ones you've been avoiding.

▲ You now have gained some flexibility, but you may feel that you've got a long way to go. In this case, you should increase the yoga flexibility portion of your program. You can do this by adding more of the yoga postures to your strength training and aerobic exercise, or by adding an extra yoga day. Continue to work on your breathing; slow down (you can increase the breath cycles up to 10 breath cycles) in each yoga pose.

▲ You may have noticed that you are tighter in your forward bending than you are in your backward bending, or vice versa. Practice will lessen this difference.

▲ You may find yourself avoiding backward bending. Remind yourself you're not getting better at doing this by avoiding it. Learn to love it.

▲ You may have noticed that you are tighter on one side than the other. Keep incorporating the twisting postures; work on relaxing more into them so they "loosen" up.

▲ You find yourself still struggling with the balancing poses. Don't avoid them, but keep practicing and work with the complementary strength training exercises to strengthen the key muscle groups involved. You will get better and better.

▲ If you have been avoiding the inversions partly or entirely (unless for medical or physical reasons), try to work on processing the fear involved in turning yourself upside-down.

Strength Training

▲ You may feel you've gained a lot of strength, but you still find the arm balancing poses challenging, especially the Chaturanga. Keep increasing the resistance in your strength training to increase your muscular power. You might also increase your repetitions; for example, if you are doing two sets, you might need to increase to three sets. You might also try increasing the resistance within your two sets and decrease your repetitions to between 8 and 12 reps. If you are doing one exercise per body part, you might want to increase to two exercises per body part.

▲ You have gained strength on your weaker side, but you are still weaker on one side than the other. Continue to work your weaker side with the single-side stabilization exercises.

▲ You notice a change in your muscle tone, but you can still see cellulite. Continue the targeted exercises such as the leg extension and the leg curl. If you have been doing two sets, you might want to increase to three sets, or increase the resistance within your two sets.

▲ You notice a change in your muscle tone, but you want more tone and definition. Continue increasing the resistance. If you are doing one exercise per body part, increase to two exercises per body part.

▲ Your body is in better proportion, but you would like it to improve even more. If you are bottom-heavy, continue to work your lower body as you have been, but increase your upper body work to create better symmetry. Continue working your lower body to downsize by toning up areas that accumulate fat. Increased muscle mass and definition in your upper body and shoulders create the illusion that your hips are smaller.

Aerobic Endurance

▲ Your resting heart rate has gone down since you started, giving you reinforcement that you are working within the correct target heart rate zone. You might not need to increase the duration, but continue to increase the intensity.

▲ Your resting heart rate has not gone down a lot since you started, indicating that you're not working hard enough. Adjust your target heart rate zone to increase the intensity of your workouts.

▲ You are bored with your endurance workouts. Change your routine by adding the aerobic exercises you have not already done, incorporating interval training, or taking your workouts outside if you've been exercising inside.

▲ If you are having a hard time increasing muscle mass you might be doing too much endurance training. The workout is draining your energy rather than giving you energy. Decrease your endurance training and put more time into your strength training and yoga flexibility.

What You Can Accomplish Now

The sky is the limit, really. At this point, make sure you don't change your program drastically. Remember, you have only been doing each level for 4 weeks, which is not a very long time.

Be open to changes and be willing to adjust and adapt yourself according to how your body responds. Be creative, be open, take in what you need, and leave out what doesn't work. Don't be afraid to change. This is how to stay motivated. Look at what you have accomplished so far! Look how far you have come in just 2 to 3 months—imagine how much farther you can go.

Resource Guide

Here are some reliable and affordable places where I order equipment and where I advise clients to go:

▲ Stability balls, tubing, free weights: www.fitnesswholesale.com

STABILITY BALL

The balls range from 45 cm to 85 cm; make sure to choose a ball that fits your body height. Use the chart I've provided under Levels 2 and 3 strength training. You can save money when you buy a stability ball without the retail box.

TUBING

There are four different resistances: fuchsia (light), yellow (medium), teal (hard), and silver (very hard). Choose the resistance that will work for you and the body part you're working. This particular company offers two types of handles, plastic and cushioned. I recommend the cushioned handle since it gives a better grip.

FREE WEIGHTS

There are several types of free weights. You can get solid metal dumbbells, solid metal dumbbells coated in vibrant colored vinyl, and solid metal dumbbells dipped in neoprene. Choose the type that you prefer. I recommend you have a range of free weights weighing from five to (at least) ten pounds.

▲ Yoga mats/straps/blocks: www.bheka.com

MAT

The Standard Long Life Mat is my favorite yoga mat because it has excellent traction without being too sticky. It comes in several colors, is 24" wide, 2mm thick ($^1/_8$"), and 69" long. For those over 6 feet in height, a 74" long mat is also available.

For those who prefer extra padding in a yoga mat, check out the Deluxe Long Life Yoga Mat. It has the same excellent traction and durability as the standard yoga mat but is almost twice as thick. The Deluxe Long Life Yoga Mat is 4mm thick ($^3/_{16}$") and 24" wide, and is also available in 69" and 74".

STRAP

The cotton straps are available in two widths: wide (1.5") and narrow (1"). The wide straps are made in 6-, 8-, and 9-foot lengths. For the purpose of this book, a wide 6- or 8-foot-long strap should be sufficient.

BLOCK

There are three types of yoga blocks: wood, and two types of foam (charcoal and purple). The purple blocks are slightly firmer than the charcoal. Either one is fine for the purposes of this book.

▲ Mysore practice rug:

If you find you perspire a lot or you need extra traction, an excellent practice tool is the Mysore practice rug available at: www.barefootyoga.com. Use the rug over a yoga mat for extra cushion for the seated postures and better traction and stability for the standing postures.

▲ Gripitz yoga block: www.gripitz.com

HOW TO CONTACT THE AUTHOR

Web site: www.anitagoa.com

Bibliography

Everett Aaberg, Muscle Mechanics, Human Kinetics, 1998.

American Council on Exercise (ACE), Personal Trainer Manual, second edition, American Council on Exercise (ACE), 1996.

Beryl Bender Birch, Power Yoga, Fireside, 1995.

Blandine Calais-Germain and Andree Lamotte, Anatomy of Movement Exercises, Eastland Press, 1996.

Blandine Calais-Germain, Anatomy of Movement, Eastland Press, 1993.

Michael A. Clark, Integrated Training for the New Millennium, first edition, National Academy of Sports Medicine, 2001.

Colleen Craig, Abs on the Ball, Healing Arts Press, 2003.

Frederic Delavier, Strength Training Anatomy, Human Kinetics, 2001.

T.K.V. Desikachar, The Heart of Yoga, Inner Traditions International, 1995.

Fernando Pagés Ruiz, What Science Can Teach Us About Flexibility, YogaJournal.com.

Swami Satyananada Saraswati, Asana/Pranayama/Mudra/Bandha, Bihar Yoga Bharati, Munger, Bihar, India, 1997.

John Scott, Ashtanga Yoga, first American edition, Three Rivers Press.

Wayne Westcott, Building Strength and Stamina, Human Kinetics, 2003.

Yoko Yoshikawa, Everybody Upsidedown, Yoga Journal, September/ October 2000.

Index

About the Author

Anita Goa is a certified yoga instructor and personal trainer. She teaches at two premier venues in New York City—Reebok Sports Club/NY and Sports Club/LA/NY—and serves as a personal trainer for elite athletes, entertainers, and business leaders.

Anita has appeared on *The View* and her work has been featured in leading magazines such as *Fitness, Cosmopolitan,* and *Yoga Journal.* She lives in New York City and can be reached via her website: www.anitagoa.com.